SOCIAL SAVVY
*Help your child fit in
with others*

SOCIAL SAVVY
Help your child fit in with others

LINDY PETERSEN

First published 1992 as *Stop and Think Parenting*
by Australian Council for Educational Research Ltd
This revised edition first published 2002
by Australian Council for Educational Research Ltd
19 Prospect Hill Road, Camberwell, Melbourne, Victoria, 3124

Reprinted 2003, 2006

Cover and text design by Jo Waite, Jo Waite Design
Cover photograph by Anne Menke courtesy of Getty Images
Printed by BPA Print Group

National Library of Australia Cataloguing-in-Publication data:

Petersen, Lindy.
    Social Savvy: help your child fit in with others.

Rev. ed.
ISBN 0 86431 560 0.

    1. Parenting. 2. Child rearing. 3. Social skills in
    children. I. Petersen, Lindy. Stop and think parenting.
    II. Australian Council for Educational Research. III. Title.

649.64

Visit our website: www.acerpress.com.au

Contents

Preface

Since writing the first edition of this book over 10 years ago, and with my own children 10 years older, I have come to realise that parenting is for ever. Of course, the situations you have to deal with change, the amount of control and contact you have with your children changes, but the need for your guidance and intervention at crucial times in their lives remains the same.

I have also come to realise that the STOP THINK DO method of parenting described in this book never outgrows its usefulness. Parenting really is like driving a car: once you learn to control yourself, follow a few basic road rules and practise a lot, you get better at it – even if a few accidents occur along the way!

This is a 'how-to' manual on parenting for all adults with children in their care. It teaches parents new skills for managing children, and also skills to teach children for managing others. These skills include what to say and do when faced with children's problem behaviour, how to talk and relate better with your children to avoid problems in the first place, and how to improve your children's relationships with others, including their peers and siblings. These are all skills you can learn with patience and practice.

Parenting can be a hazardous road. But you must think it is worth travelling or you wouldn't be reading this book. Most parents wish they had been better prepared before they began the journey. It is a shame children are not born with a user's manual attached! This book may in fact serve the purpose. Fortunately, it is rarely too late to learn. And your children will be better prepared when they reach parenthood because of your efforts to show and teach them good social behaviour now.

To those who have helped me travel my road, thank you ...

To my mother and father,
Mary and Tom,
for the experiences and opportunities they gave me.

To my children,
Ben and Em,
for the years of parenting practice they are still giving me.

To all the parents I have worked with
for all the lessons they have taught me.

Chapter 1

THE PARENTING ROAD

A boy runs screaming into the kitchen, clutching a trans-formable robot-cum-turtle toy. 'Peter hit me,' he cries as he clings to his mother's legs. She is chopping lettuce for lunch. An older boy storms in yelling, 'He took my robot. Give it back!' Mother sighs, 'Can't you two play for five minutes without fighting?' She knows the words off by heart. 'Why don't you both go outside until lunch is ready?' The lump on her legs whines, 'I don't want salad. I want chips.' He is distracted by his stomach. The other boy quickly grabs the toy and runs off. Mother yells after him, 'Peter, bring that back!'. He ignores her. Mother sighs again, picks up the crying child, sits him on the bench next to her... and talks about lunch.

This mother is parenting. She is caring for her children, listening and talking to them, trying to cope with their behaviour and their moods, trying to teach them things, and chopping up lettuce for their lunch. She repeats this juggling act a hundred times a day without realising what she is doing. Sometimes she feels contented; sometimes she feels completely frustrated. She wishes that she related better with her children, especially Peter. She knows she doesn't handle him well. He often says that she hates him. Sometimes she does. He is a troublesome child and she can see him growing up to be a troubled adult. She often feels quite helpless ... and he is only 10 years old. What about when he is 15? Everything outside of her seems to have much more influence on Peter – television, peers, teachers, football coaches. What about drugs? She cringes when she thinks about the pressures on children these days.

Then she reflects on her own parents. They seemed to know what to do. She may not have liked what they did, but they seemed sure. She is not. Her children are growing up in a very different world, and the ways her parents used with her just do not work with her youngsters, especially Peter. There has to be a better way that *does* work.

This mother's dilemma confronts most parents (meaning all adult caregivers) at some stage of their parenting. The fact is that parents often can't do much about the external hazards facing their children or the external pressures that affect all families at times, but they can do something about their own relationships with the children in their care, about their own skills and attitudes that they pass on to their children. If they do this well, their children will be better equipped to avoid the world's hazards for themselves.

If you are a caring parent like Peter's mother, who wants to relate well with your children and manage their behaviour better, this book has something to offer you. You will find as you read on, a common-sense method for improving your relationships as well as their behaviour. If you are a parent who is concerned about how your children get on with their brothers and sisters, cousins or friends at school, this book will provide a method for improving their social skills.

Learning this method will be like learning to drive a car. You can't just drive on impulse; you will have accidents that way. There are rules to remember and directions to follow. You will be asked to look at your own attitudes about parenting like: who has right of way, who is behind the wheel and who has the responsibility to fix things when they go wrong. And there will be traffic lights to remind you what to do along the way.

Before you take your first lesson, however, you may like to know how this book came about. As a clinical psychologist, I work daily with children, adolescents and parents who are experiencing problems in their relationships. These problems not only cause sadness and disruption in the family, but can affect children's relationships outside of the home and even their learning at school. Over the past 30 years, I have developed a method of improving relationships between parents and children, and also between children and their peers. It is also used by teachers and counsellors in schools around the world. The method is called STOP THINK DO and is the subject of this book. Hopefully, it will soon fit comfortably in your home.

The journey ahead

Let's map out the lessons ahead to reach our destination.

- Chapter 2 looks at attitudes to parenting that underlie the STOP THINK DO method. If you find that you don't share these attitudes at present, keep an open mind, read on and give the method a go. Attitudes often change with your own experiences.
- Chapter 3 teaches the STOP, THINK and DO steps using the red, yellow and green traffic lights as cues — what to do and say, and how to do and say it — when you are managing your child's troublesome behaviour. You will learn that relating with and managing children successfully requires you to STOP first, and THINK before you DO anything!
- Chapter 4 shows how to teach your children to use STOP THINK DO to solve problems they have with others. You are actually training your children's social skills at home to improve their relationships, including peer friendships.

- The Appendix contains practice exercises for your new skills. You will be guided to these exercises at the appropriate points through Chapters 3 and 4. Since this book is designed to be a practical manual, it does not contain background theory. A short list of STOP THINK DO resources is provided in the Appendix if you wish to read further on the development of this method.

Now, let's head off on our journey. You have a guide book. Move to Chapter 2 to check your attitudes to parenting and how they fit with STOP THINK DO.

Chapter 2

ATTITUDES AND IMPULSES

There is one simple rule about everything – if what you are doing works, do more of the same. But if it doesn't, try something different. Easier said than done! What keeps us doing 'more of the same' with our children, even when it doesn't work?

It is a combination of:

1. our *attitudes* to parenting, which are hard to change
2. and our *impulses,* which are hard to control.

In this chapter, we will discuss some of the attitudes and impulses that govern your parenting. They may need a tune-up and some adjustment if STOP THINK DO is to run smoothly in your family.

You are totally responsible ... Wrong!

Probably the most important attitude for learner drivers to consider is who is responsible for what on the roads. And, as a parent, you need to consider who is responsible for what in your family. Encouraging your children to take responsibility and giving up some of your own is critical to STOP THINK DO, and critical for you if you want it to work in your family.

Many parents feel that they are responsible for everything that happens in the family because they are adults. They believe that they have sole authority and power for making decisions and solving problems that arise in the family. The roots of this view run deep. It is consistent with the old autocratic parenting style in which many parents were themselves raised. Parents were the bosses and they dealt out rewards and punishments to make their children do what they wanted. They felt strong, and sure of what they were doing, and their techniques often worked in the short term.

However over recent decades, there has been a dramatic change in the society in which our children are growing up. These old attitudes do not fit comfortably with democratic beliefs in equality and respect for all individuals, regardless of sex, race, status, religion or indeed, age. Our children are learning that no one has the right to impose anything on anyone else. They will resent and resist those who try, including their parents. But, if they cannot make their children do anything, how can caring parents guide their children through happy and responsible childhood into happy and responsible adulthood?

The STOP THINK DO method of parenting is one way. It is based on the attitude that both parents and children have *rights* to make decisions and choices about matters that affect them, and they have the *responsibility* to take part in making those decisions and experiencing the consequences. Most schools these days adopt a similar democratic approach to discipline and education in general. Thus, parents using STOP THINK DO at home are helping their children prepare for this approach at school.

In truth, most parents don't consciously choose any particular way of parenting. Instead, they swing between being the boss, being the wimp and being the equal, depending on the circumstances and their mood. Most parents are not consistent. This is why their techniques work sometimes and not others. While you are learning

STOP THINK DO, you will become more aware of what you *are* doing with your children, and why it may not be working. You will also become aware of the benefits of sharing the rights and responsibilities of living in a family with your children. Using this method, your children may seem to have more rights than they did previously in your family, but they will also have more responsibilities. This may be rather threatening at first. But after a while, you will realise that it is such a relief to share the driving on a long trip.

You are responsible for their relations ... Wrong!

Even when parents are not directly involved, they feel that they *must* intervene in their children's affairs with other people, especially if there are problems. This is particularly true when brothers and sisters or friends are involved in hassles. Parents hate to see their children hurt, unhappy or unconfident, and they develop a habit of interceding on their behalf from an early age. Children come to rely on their parents to solve their problems and often hook them in for just this purpose. It is really no surprise that some children fail to develop confidence and maturity in their social life when their parents have generally lived it for them.

With STOP THINK DO, you have a way of helping your children relate better with others, but not by taking over their relationships or problems. By teaching your children to use the method themselves with other people, you are teaching them to take responsibility for themselves, and you are teaching them the skills they need to do so. You can guide them through the steps but where they end up in their journey with other people is their business, their responsibility. They are behind the wheel; you navigate. It may take quite a shift in your attitude to be a navigator rather than a back-seat driver in your child's social life.

It's not what you say, it's what you do ... Wrong!

Imagine yourself in heavy traffic, trying to park your car. How do you feel when the driver next to you winds down his window to let you know exactly what he thinks about you and your driving? Does it help you be a better driver? Worse still, imagine yourself in the same situation when you were a learner driver, unskilled and unsure. The words of the other driver would really hurt then – you probably felt like giving up, crying or hitting back.

In many ways, children are always in this situation – learners in everything. Children cannot do things as well as adults; they do not have the skills or experience. They will gain these if they are given encouragement for their efforts rather than criticism for their failures. The most powerful way of encouraging children is through what is said to them and how it is said. If parents are honest, they will admit that they often communicate anything but encouragement and respect to their children. In their haste and frustration, they often criticise, nag, order, beg, embarrass and put down their children, just like the driver did when you were trying to park. And their children probably give up, cry or hit back as well. Indeed, professionals who work with families generally believe that the language and tone of voice parents use with their children is the most critical factor affecting relationships in the home.

STOP THINK DO is a vehicle that runs on the fuel of good, positive talk and communication between parents and children. And, it should be regularly topped up. Here are some ideas to use everyday:

- Tell your children what they are doing well.
  Don't tell them what they can't do. After all, they are only learners and there are lots of things they can't do.
- Tell them how they are improving at something, or really trying. Don't wait for everything to be done perfectly before you say something.

- Use the same tone of voice with your children as you want them to use with you. Remember how the other driver made you feel when you were trying to park: you don't want your children to feel like that when you speak to them.

You may find that generally talking more positively to your children and also 'watching your mouth' (what you say and how you say it) when you have issues with their behaviour can reduce the likelihood of misbehaviour occurring in the first place. Children whose parents generally talk respectfully to them and about them don't need to gain their parent's attention in negative ways. They learn to talk through matters maturely and openly rather than act out their feelings in negative behaviour or bottling them inside as emotional stress.

Yes, it certainly does matter what you say to your children and how you say it. If you have trouble remembering this, picture an 'L' plate around your child's neck ... and speak accordingly.

You should treat your children the same ... Right!

Certainly you should treat your children the same when it comes to managing problem behaviour. If someone secretly taped you at home when you are managing your children, I can guarantee you would be very surprised (and probably embarrassed) about how you look and sound. You and your partner might like to do this to each other – it will change your life! But what would most surprise you is how differently you sound and act with your different children. I believe that this variation is largely due to personality differences: you naturally clash with some personalities and not others. This accounts for the fact that you are more successful in management with one child than the other, yet it might be the other way round for your partner, who has a different personality again.

Let's look at some personality styles and see if you can identify them in your family. In Chapter 3, you will be meeting several of these characters. Some children are quite dependent, needy of attention and parental involvement. They constantly 'pull in' attention from parents, using positive or negative means. If this style is particularly annoying to a parent and 'grates on their personality', the parent is likely to respond emotionally. These emotional 'pulling' sessions become a bad habit between parent and child, and problems between them are not likely to get resolved easily. Unfortunately, the parent's reactions actually feed the child's immature, dependent personality and behaviour.

Other children have power personalities. They need to maintain control in their life and 'push away' parents to have the last say themselves. If this style grates on a parent or the parent also has a power personality and wants to have the last say, the parent is likely to react emotionally and engage in 'pushing' power struggles with a child like this. Problems between them are not likely to be resolved easily. The parent in fact feeds their child's defiant personality. The most difficult children to manage are those with a strong mix of dependent and power traits: they 'pull in' their parents for needy attention and then 'push away' to do things their way in the end. Even little issues can become major problems with these intense children. This makes consistent management very difficult, especially by inconsistent parents, as we all are at times.

Obviously, parents or children can't simply change their personalities. But if personality differences are so important, how can parents ever hope to be more effective and consistent with their children? There is an answer in STOP THINK DO. By using this method for managing *all* children in the family, the personality differences won't matter. Parents use the same words and actions with all of their children. They even use the same tone of voice: a low and slow voice tone is the one children listen to best, and it is not emotionally provocative, meaning that it is not likely to feed negative personality traits or habits in individual children. There is another benefit of using the same words and voice with all members of the family: children will not feel they are being singled out or picked on personally. Everyone is being treated the same, just as the rules of the road apply equally to everyone.

Parents must agree on parenting ... Wrong!

In an ideal world, parents in a family would agree with the principles and practices of a positive parenting method like STOP THINK DO, and be consistent with each other in their management of the children. However, in the real world, parents are individuals with different personalities and life experiences, and will not always agree on how to manage the children's behaviour, whatever the methods being tried. Fortunately, children are quite flexible beings and they can learn to live with inconsistencies between the attitudes and behaviours of their parents. After all, they have to learn to adapt to a variety of care-giving styles over their lives – within their extended family, blended families, sporting teams, social and school environments.

So, if you are determined to try STOP THINK DO to manage the children and your partner is not interested or negative, I suggest that you still adopt the method in your own dealings with the children. You can still reap the benefits in terms of improved relationships with your children. It is an idea to ask your partner for passive support: that is, ask them not to interfere with your management strategies. If your partner does interfere and undermine your efforts at times, I suggest that you do not argue with them in front of the children. Talk about it later and reach a compromise if possible. Children will play parents off against each other if they perceive such conflicts between them. Also, remember that you are trying to demonstrate and teach your children a positive method for solving problems with others, so you cannot be seen to be involved in negative arguments with your partner. You need to practise what you preach! Interestingly, when sceptical parents see positive changes occurring in their children due to their partner's new methods, they are often converted.

Even if both parents in a family are keen to try STOP THINK DO, they will still have differences in their level of skill and commitment at various times. If one parent is having difficulty following the steps or is 'losing it' in a problem situation with the children, they may invite the other parent to take over, or both parents may leave the children to work it out ... and go and take a rest break. It is handy to have a few support drivers to call on.

Patience is a virtue ... Right!

If only the other driver had this attitude when you were trying to park! Impatience leads to loss of control on the road and in the home. Parents need to be cool, calm and collected in order to think clearly and avoid potential hazards. This is particularly true for parents who are still learning STOP THINK DO. While you remain patient with your children and with yourselves, you will actually have more control and more influence in your family. Your impulses will not lead you to make mistakes. You will avoid head-on collisions with your children's personalities. And, you will model the very process you are trying to teach your children to use with others, namely that there are always answers to problems if they stay clam and clear thinking. Children discover that the benefits of this patient, problem-solving attitude apply to many areas of life in and out of the home. It is helpful when handling schoolwork, authority figures, employers, friendships – and when learning to drive a car themselves.

Right now, though, you will need to be most patient with yourself. You're only a learner of this new method. If you are trying STOP THINK DO with your child on a particular occasion and you feel yourself becoming frustrated and impatient, take a break – put it back to your child to work it out and/or just leave it until you are composed and ready to try again. It may sound too hard at the moment. But, if you consider the amount of time you spend daily relating with and managing your children, the promise of a more effective way that can also improve your children's social behaviour generally has got to be worth a try. So, don't worry... be patient!

We all need reminding ... Right!

This is especially true when we are learning something new. STOP THINK DO uses a powerful reminder to help you be patient and learn the rules: the traffic light. On the road, traffic lights slow you down, give you time to reflect on the rules of the road and remind you of what to do to stay safe and also protect others. The red light cues you to STOP and wait, the yellow light cues you to think about where you are going and to get ready to move, and the green light cues you to go ahead. And if you follow these steps, driving is more likely to be smooth, safe and rewarding.

The same applies on the parenting road. The red light reminds you and your children to STOP first when you have problems; the yellow light cues you to THINK about what you could do; and the green light tells you to choose something and DO it! To reinforce the steps in your home, you and your children could make up a traffic light out of coloured cardboard to display – as a reminder for everyone.

Summary: Attitudes to develop and impulses to control

- Share the rights and responsibilities of family membership with your children. The only way they will learn to respect other people's rights or to be responsible for themselves is if you let them practise at home, even if they make mistakes.

- You can't make your children do anything in today's democratic world. You can change your own attitudes and behaviour, which will bring about change in theirs.

- Don't take over your children's relationships with others: they will never learn how to do it. Instead, teach them STOP THINK DO to use with others.

- Watch your mouth. How you talk to your children will make or break your attempts to use STOP THINK DO. Generally talk positively and respectfully.

- Use the same words, actions and tone of voice (low and slow) with all your children when you are managing behaviour problems. You will avoid personality clashes and children taking the things you say personally. This method applies equally to all.

- Learners need encouragement. Your children are always learners by virtue of their age and inexperience, and need your encouragement. And, as a learner of this new parenting method, frequently encourage yourself to keep trying.
- Impulses cause accidents. Calmness, patience and clear thinking are the main rules of effective parenting. The aim of STOP THINK DO is essentially to take emotional impulses out of behaviour management, and teach parents and children to use their brains instead.

- Traffic lights remind you to be patient on the road and follow the rules. They also remind you to be patient in the management of your children and follow the rules of STOP THINK DO.

In Chapter 3, you will learn the STOP THINK DO steps for managing children's behaviour in detail – what to do and say when you have a problem with your child.

Chapter 3

Managing children's behaviour

When you are faced with your child's misbehaviour, the red traffic light reminds you to STOP first before you do anything.
At STOP, there are two steps:

- Step 1 is to STOP yourself reacting impulsively. Just look and listen to what is actually happening.
- Step 2 is to STOP yourself from expressing your feelings the wrong way. State your feelings about the problem clearly and calmly.

Step 1: STOP, look and listen

The STOP steps are the hardest of all to learn. STOP goes against our natural impulses and often, our ingrained attitudes about parenting. Usually when there are problems, parents jump in quickly with comments, answers and directions. They react out of habit. The most difficult thing for them to do is nothing!

Yet this is precisely what parents are required to do at the STOP stage. When your child's behaviour is a problem, STOP yourself before you rush into anything, before you react on impulse. This is the time for finding out information to help you decide what to do. You are not ready to DO anything yet. Remember, the red light is on!

Why STOP?

You may be wondering why is it not a good policy to react impulsively to children's behaviour. There are many reasons. The main ones are:

- When parents react quickly, they do so because they assume they know what happened and why: they guess on the basis of their past experiences with their children. They may not have seen what happened on that particular occasion, yet they intervene. But parents can make mistakes this way. For example, they may blame the wrong child, who then develops a role as the victim in the family and a need to constantly defend themselves. By stopping first to look and listen carefully to the facts of the situation, parents are less likely to make mistakes. This is not the time for guesswork.

- When parents react quickly, they tend to get emotional themselves: they resort to techniques like begging, yelling, arguing, criticising, putting down, preaching, smacking. They are not good models for their children to copy! Why should children learn to control their feelings and behaviour if their parents act like 'fruitcakes' when faced with problems? Children will naturally become upset, defensive or aggressive if their parents are behaving this way.

- When parents react quickly, they generally talk too much, especially 'emotional talk'. Over the decades I have worked with families, I have concluded that children get accustomed to their parent's voice and switch off after about word three in a sentence, especially if the parent is prone to nagging, preaching or yelling.

If parents want children to listen to them, they need to choose their words wisely and deliver them calmly.

- When parents react quickly, they give too much attention to negative behaviour, which unfortunately reinforces it. Every child has a natural need for attention from their parents, to feel as if they belong to them. This need varies considerably amongst children in terms of how strong it is and how it is manifested in their behaviour. While children do want to behave in ways that please their parents, often they find that behaving in ways that displease their parents gets them even more attention. They are likely to repeat these behaviours in the future because they worked in the past to flag parent's attention.

Summarising the reasons why you should STOP yourself from reacting quickly when your child behaves in a way which displeases you:
- you *could* be making a big mistake
- you *are* likely to overreact emotionally so why shouldn't they?
- you *are* likely to be switched off by them so it won't work anyway
- you *are* reinforcing their misbehaviour by giving it attention so the misbehaviour *is* likely to continue or occur again.

These are the most common parenting errors I see in normal families. They can lead to serious accidents as the following examples demonstrate.

Accidents caused by not stopping

Below are some examples of typical problem situations that occur in families, and typical impulsive reactions by parents in their attempts to solve these problems. These impulsive, emotional reactions rarely work, and can even make the problem worse or cause serious accidents with long-term consequences. The same examples will be followed through the STOP, THINK and DO steps, so you can trace what to do and what not to do from beginning to end of each story.

Susan's shoes

Impulsive reactions by parents often reinforce their children's immaturity as did Susan's mother.

> *The mother of six-year-old Susan called to her daughter to hurry and put her shoes on. They were late getting ready for an appointment with the dentist. Susan dawdled out of her room. She was sobbing because she could not find her shoes. Her mother gave an exasperated sigh, whined at Susan and rushed into the room to look for the shoes. Susan sat down and watched television while she waited for her mother.*

The following questions help us understand what happened in this situation.

What did the child actually do?	Could not find her shoes, cried.
What did the parent assume?	Child is helpless, needs assistance.
What did the parent feel?	Frustrated, despairing.
How did the parent immediately react?	Rushed to look for shoes.
How did the child respond?	Waited for mother to find shoes.

Susan's mother did not STOP, look and listen to work out the actual problem on this occasion, namely that Susan did not have her shoes. Instead, mother made a quick assumption that Susan was behaving in her usual helpless manner, felt frustrated and annoyed, then reacted to her 'helpless' child by looking for the shoes herself. Susan's response – watching television while her mother found her shoes – simply reinforced her view (and her mother's) that she was indeed inadequate and needed her mother's help.

What will happen next time? Susan is learning that she can gain her mother's attention and service by behaving helplessly. And she will continue behaving this way. It is also feeding her naturally dependent personality. Moreover, Susan's mother is inadvertently giving her daughter a vote of 'no confidence' by her actions and her words. She is giving Susan the message that she does not believe Susan could get her shoes herself. Children like Susan only take on more responsibilities and become more independent if they get the message from their parents that they believe *she* can do it, not that she is a baby and needs their help all the time!

Many parents typically operate like Susan's mother, doing things for their children when they are capable of doing it themselves. Parents opt for short-term gains like getting places on time or having chores done properly, but pay long-term penalties of dependent and inadequate children. Of course, Susan's mother may find the shoes and keep the appointment, thus satisfying her needs in the short term. However, at what price? She has set herself up to be in her daughter's service for a long time to come. Her feelings of frustration and even resentment of Susan will remain while she continues to rush in and help her whenever she seems to need it. She will pay a penalty for not STOPPING at the red light when problems first arise.

Roberto's bike

Impulsive reactions can turn a parent-child conflict into a head-on collision as in the next example.

> *Twelve-year-old Roberto raced home from school, dropping his bike in the driveway. His stepfather yelled from the shed for him not to be so careless, and to put the bike away immediately or else ... Roberto became angry and complained that his stepfather always picked on him. Roberto challenged him to make him shift the bike. At this point, father became very angry and stormed out of the shed towards Roberto, who ran off, leaving the bike on the drive.*

The following questions help us understand what happened here:

What did the child actually do?	Left his bike on the driveway.
What did the parent assume?	Child is irresponsible and defiant.
What did the parent feel?	Angry, challenged.
How did the parent immediately react?	Yelled, ordered, put child down.
How did the child respond?	Challenged father again, ran off.

When Roberto left his bike on the driveway, his stepfather did not STOP, look and listen to work out what was really happening. Instead, he assumed that this was an example of Roberto's typically irresponsible, defiant behaviour, which made him angry and determined not to let his stepson get away with it. Father reacted impulsively to what he assumed about Roberto's motives. He did not deal at all with the actual problem, namely, the bike on the driveway.

What will happen next time? Roberto is learning that a guaranteed method of getting attention and even power in the family is to challenge his stepfather, to threaten his power and authority ... then he will surely react. By not STOPPING before he reacted on impulse and assumption, Roberto's father actually reinforced a power struggle between himself and his stepson. No doubt, this situation could spill over into a conflict between Roberto's mother and his stepfather as the latter tries to establish some credibility in his parenting role with Roberto while his mother gets torn between the two!

And, what happened to the bike? This parent did not even get his short-term goal met − getting the bike off the driveway − let alone long-term goals like teaching his stepson to be more responsible in potentially dangerous situations, or developing a respectful relationship with him. What a serious mistake this father made by not stopping.

Tyson's television

Impulsive reactions by parents can be quite confusing to their children, as in the following example:

> *Three-year-old Tyson repeatedly wandered in front of the television set while his mother was watching her favourite program. With a mischievous grin on his face, he banged his hands on the screen, then looked at his mother. She begged him to get out of the way and to give her a few minutes peace. Finally, she smacked him on the legs. He fell to the floor in front of the television set and began to scream. Mother picked him up and nursed him while she continued to watch her program.*

Let's look at the situation in detail:

What did the child actually do?	Stood in front of the television.
What did the parent assume?	Child is demanding and trying to stop her doing what she wants.
What did the parent feel?	Irritated, imposed upon.
How did the parent immediately react?	Begged, smacked the child.
How did the child respond?	Fell to the floor, screamed.

This mother did not deal well with her little boy's problem behaviour. She did not look and listen to what he was actually doing. Instead, she became frustrated and annoyed because she assumed that her son was being demanding as usual, never allowing her time to herself. She then reacted by giving him the attention he was demanding! She begged, then smacked and finally nursed him to satisfy her short-term goal of seeing her television program.

What will happen the next time this mother sits down to watch television? Unfortunately, she will pay a long-term price for her impulsive reactions. Tyson is learning at a young age that he can hook his mother in by behaving in certain ways – standing in front of the television set, falling to the ground, screaming. Even smacks constitute attention and are reinforcing to the child, especially when followed by a confusing cuddle. His mother has inadvertently increased her son's repertoire of attention-seeking behaviours, and his confusion about her feelings and behaviour. Tyson is learning to temper tantrum!

Clara's allowance

Teenagers are particularly sensitive to impulsive reactions from their parents. Consider the following story.

> Sixteen-year-old Clara had spent her allowance for the week. She really wanted to go to the local disco, so she asked her parents for an advance. Her father immediately accused her of wasting her money, probably on drugs like all her useless friends. He declared that he would not be used by his daughter this way. Clara got upset. She accused her parents of being mean and untrusting. As she stormed out of the kitchen, she vowed to make them sorry. On the night of the disco, Clara told her parents that she was staying with her girlfriend. Instead, she took money from her mother's purse and went to the disco.

Let's retrace the sequence of events leading to this unhappy end:

What did the child actually do?	Asked for money for the disco.
What did the parents assume?	Child is a useless teenager who squanders her money, is on drugs and uses her parents.
What did the parents feel?	Concerned, 'got at', resentful.
How did the parents immediately react?	Put down, accused the child.

How did the child respond?   Put down, accused parents,
                                                lied, stole from parents.

Unfortunately, this scene typifies many child-parent interactions
when the children have reached adolescence. There are elements of
retaliation, of getting back, with the child feeling unfairly treated,
and the parent feeling hurt and resentful. None of this is justified
when you look at what really happened. Clara only asked for an
advance on her allowance. Her father did not STOP to listen to the
actual problem. He reacted to what he thought he knew, what he
guessed about his daughter, and her friends, and all teenagers.

Clara's father may consider that he achieved his goal, namely, to
avoid being used by his daughter and to make the point about use-
less teenagers. However, the repair bill on his relationship with his
daughter may be too high a price to pay. Clara is learning the game
of 'one-upmanship', of retaliation and revenge. This game is likely
to continue and even become more intense and nasty as parent and
child seek to 'up' the other in many such situations. And neither
party would accept responsibility for this dilemma: they are only
reacting to the other party.

If Clara carried over these attitudes and this game into other areas
of her life, she may have difficulty coping with conflict and authority
outside of the home as well. The need to retaliate and 'get even' is
strong in adolescents who show anti-social, delinquent behaviour
like vandalising or stealing. This sad scenario may be avoided if
Clara's parents STOP themselves from reacting on impulse, and look
at each situation as it happens.

Your reactions

Look at situations in your home. Take some time to think about the
way you react to your child's behaviour. Recall a particular problem.
Ask yourself the following questions and record your answers. Read
both questions on each line before answering:

	Yes/No		Yes/No
Did I observe what actually happened?		OR did I assume I knew what happened?	
Did I deal with what I saw and heard?		OR did I act on my assumptions and guesses?	
Did I think at all about how to handle the situation?		OR did I feel frustrated, annoyed, angry, irritated, hurt or resentful – and just react accordingly?	
Did I allow my child to take responsibility for solving the problem?		OR did I immediately react to solve the problem myself?	
Did I consider long-term goals like developing my child's sense of responsibility and confidence?		OR did I only consider short-term gains like resolving the issue quickly myself?	
Did I handle the behaviour effectively so that it is not likely to happen again?		OR, by jumping in quickly, did I actually reinforce the behaviour by giving it emotional attention so that it is likely to happen again?	

If you answered 'yes' to some of the questions in the left column, you are already stopping yourself, at least sometimes. You are well on the way to managing your child's behaviour more effectively. If you answered 'yes' to questions in the right column, you are reacting impulsively and emotionally to your child and are probably feeding their misbehaviour with your attention. Put simply, to discourage misbehaviour, STOP responding to it on impulse! Stopping is your insurance policy against accidents and damage caused when parents react impulsively and emotionally to their children's behaviour.

Summary: How to STOP, look and listen at Step 1

How to STOP yourself when you are so used to reacting quickly to your children ...

- Remember the red traffic light. Put red circles of cardboard around the house to remind you to STOP first when you have a problem with their behaviour.

- Physically take a step back from the problem situation, go to the toilet, put on a walkman radio, count to five, tell yourself to keep calm – whatever it takes to compose and control yourself (unless someone is in immediate physical danger).

- Don't make assumptions about why your child is misbehaving.

- Don't say or do anything to your child.

- Use only your eyes and ears to work out what is actually happening – what it is that your child is doing or saying that is causing you the problem.

Practice

For practice in the first STOP step – STOP, look and listen to find out what is happening in problem situations – try the exercise in Appendix 1. Then, move on to the second STOP step where you stop yourself from expressing your feelings the wrong way.

Step 2: Express your feelings honestly

Our feelings are what drive our behaviour. We saw this very clearly in the problem situations described in Step 1. These parents felt irritated, worried, frustrated, angry or resentful in response to the behaviour of their children. We may agree that it is natural for these parents to have these feelings in the circumstances; they're only human. But how they communicated their feelings is the problem. Most people believe that it is good to talk about your feelings, unhealthy to bottle them up inside and painful to act them out on others. These parents acted out their feelings on their children by yelling, putting down, begging, smacking, ordering or giving in. It did not solve the immediate problem and worse, it dirtied the fuel-line to good relationships with their children in the longer term. Indeed, the most harm was probably done by what came out of the parent's mouth!

Impulsive 'You' messages

When parents react quickly and impulsively to their children's behaviour, they generally throw 'You' messages at their children. These are emotional statements that stem from their feelings, but, instead of expressing them clearly and honestly, just blame the child. They say how bad or inadequate the child is – 'you' are the problem – and they don't even mention the parent's feelings. Nor do they mention the particular problem: they are just about the child and what is wrong with him or her.

How is the child supposed to handle these messages? They cannot change their entire personality on the spot! 'You' messages are always taken personally and reacted to emotionally. They breed more 'You' messages because they contain blame and criticism, which raise emotions in the listener, who has to respond to defend themself. Often, the original problem is left unresolved, real feelings left unexpressed and the listener left emotionally confused. Indeed, children are not likely to change their behaviour or solve problems with parents under these conditions. The examples from Step 1 demonstrate the hopelessness, confusion and damage that result when feelings are not expressed clearly.

Susan's shoes

In her rush to find her daughter's shoes, imagine that Susan's mother expressed her feelings of frustration and annoyance in this 'You' message:

> '**You** really are hopeless, Susan. Will **you** ever grow up?'

Although this statement is driven by mother's feelings, it doesn't mention mother or her feelings at all. And it doesn't tell Susan what she has actually done. Instead, it puts Susan down as a person. What is she supposed to do in response? She can't change her whole personality and grow up on the spot! So, Susan is likely to react defensively to protect herself. She becomes more upset and sobs an emotional 'You' message back to her mother:

> '**You** must have taken them. **You** never do anything for me.'

As her mother did to her, Susan is taking her feelings out on her mother rather than expressing them honestly. I imagine that mother's next statement to Susan is likely to be another 'You' message. They are becoming locked into a habit. And on it goes ... a spiral of negative communication. I hardly think that Susan and her mother will work together to get to the dentist either.

Clara's allowance

Clara's father was no doubt very concerned about what was happening to Clara's budget. He may also have been frustrated when asked for money again. But he impulsively expressed his feelings in 'You' messages that said nothing about his feelings or the actual problem of the money. He said:

> *'What's the matter with **you**? **You** must be on drugs.*
> ***You** teenagers waste your money these days.'*

His true feelings of concern and frustration were hidden as he put his
daughter down, tore her character apart, and preached about the
general problem of youth and drugs today. What is she supposed to
do now? She cannot change herself, her friends and the whole teenage
population on the spot! Because Clara was confused by his message
and felt personally attacked, she naturally defended herself and
responded with more 'You' messages:

> *'**You** don't care about me anyway.*
> ***You** are the meanest parents in the world.'*

And father was hurt by this personal attack. He responded with more
'You' messages:

> *'How dare **you** talk to your parents like that!*
> *That's another thing about **you** teenagers – no respect for your elders.*
> ***You're** not going to get a cent from me!'*

And Clara answered:

> *'**You'll** be sorry!'*

And the door is slammed shut. This parent-child relationship is in
big trouble.

Roberto's bike and Tyson's television

As a practice exercise (although we usually don't need practice in
'You' messages – we're skilled enough!), try constructing 'You' messages for the stories about Roberto and Tyson. For instance,
Roberto's stepfather, who felt very angry, might react impulsively
with the message:

> *'You're so careless. Are you trying to kill somebody?*
> *You don't deserve a bike.'*

Father did not mention his feelings or the actual problem of the bike on the driveway. He just attacked Roberto's character. What can the boy do about his whole character? Guess some 'You' messages that Roberto is now likely to use on his father to defend himself. Do you think the problem of the bike on the driveway is likely to be solved now?

Or Tyson's mother might say in her frustration over missing her TV program:

> *'Won't you please go away? You never give me any peace.*
> *You are driving me crazy.'*

While Tyson may not understand the words she is using, he will pick up his mother's negative tone of voice and the fact that he is being blamed. Tyson will learn to do the same back to her in a few more months. Think of some 'You' messages that you hear coming from even very young children. By not stopping first in our reactions to our children when they misbehave, we unfortunately make it very easy for them to learn 'You' messages from us.

Honest 'I' messages

If 'You' messages, are ineffective and even harmful, how can parents express their feelings to their children? The answer is 'I' messages. These are honest statements about feelings that do not blame or discourage the child. Often children are so engrossed in their own business and meeting their own needs that they are not aware of how their behaviour affects other people. 'I' messages let them know. 'I' messages follow the formula:

> *'I feel* (state feeling) *because* (state problem)'

Worry, sadness, concern, disappointment, frustration, fear and anger can be communicated unambiguously by using words to describe the basic feeling, a serious facial expression to match the feeling, and by stating the problem that is the reason for the feeling. They can also describe the strength of the feeling, for example a *little* disappointed or *very* disappointed. All this can be expressed in an 'I' message, often without referring to the child, and certainly without blaming them.

Here is a road warning. Beware of Angry 'I' messages: they begin with 'I' but end up as 'You' messages that blame and put down the child personally. For instance, *'I feel angry because **you** are so useless/irresponsible/rude/painful'*. Sometimes anger is not the feeling you really need to express anyway. Behind anger is often a more basic emotion like embarrassment, fear or worry. This was the case when the 13-year-old returned home late one night and his mother screamed this Angry 'I' message:

> *'**I'm** so mad at you. **You** just do this to upset me. **You're** so irresponsible.'*

Mother was quick to express her anger, yet her honest feelings were hidden. Basically, she was worried about her son, fearful for his safety and eventually relieved when he returned home. Her statements missed these feelings. The result was probably a confused, angry and upset child, and very little chance of working out a solution for next time he went out. An honest 'I' message would express these primary feelings:

> *'**I** feel very worried when you are out late.*
> ***I'm** afraid something has happened to you.*
> ***I'm** so relieved when you get home.'*

In response, the child is less likely to feel angry or confused, and more likely to understand his mother's feelings and want to relieve

her stress next time he goes out. 'I' messages may not actually solve
problems, but they do not offend and therefore keep the lines of communication open to find answers.

Avoid accidents with 'I' messages

Refer again to the familiar examples from Step 1 to see how these
parents could STOP themselves from impulsively reacting with
potentially lethal 'You' messages, and instead express their basic
feelings honestly in 'I' messages so the door remains open to solve
the problem at hand.

Susan's shoes

Say Susan's mother STOPPED herself from reacting impulsively and
from giving an emotional 'You' message to her daughter. Instead,
she took a deep breath and calmed herself. She watched what Susan
was doing and heard what she was saying (Step 1). Since it was
important for her to keep this appointment, Susan being without her
shoes was a problem for her. She approached Susan with a serious
look on her face and expressed her feelings about this situation in an
'I' message (Step 2).

> *'I feel very annoyed because we have an appointment in 15 minutes
> and we cannot leave without your shoes.'*

Susan's mother clearly stated the problem and her feelings using
words that also conveyed the intensity she felt – *very* annoyed. Susan
was not blamed, she was just told. The message should be quite clear
to her about how her mother feels and what is the actual problem
causing her to feel this way. And she *can* do something about her
shoes; she is not being challenged to change her whole personality
on the spot.

Indeed, Susan is almost committed to finding a solution. When
face-to-face with her mother, who is showing self-control, clarity of
thought, careful observation of the situation, open expression of

feelings and a respectful tone, it would be very difficult for Susan to deny responsibility ('you must have taken my shoes') or to claim ignorance of the problem ('I didn't hear you tell me to find my shoes'). She is obliged to consider the problem and her mother's feelings. Also, by not behaving emotionally, mother is demonstrating or modelling self-control and responsible behaviour for Susan, who is likely to act the same. The doors are open for more talk and more answers.

Roberto's bike

When Roberto left his bike on the driveway, his stepfather felt angry. But he STOPPED himself from rushing into anything, and from giving Roberto the 'You' (or Angry 'I') message that was on the tip of his tongue (Step 1). Rather, he looked at the situation, walked up to his stepson and expressed his true feelings about the problem (Step 2).

> *'I am really worried about bikes left on the driveway.*
> *They can cause accidents.'*

This is an honest statement of fact and feeling that should leave Roberto in no doubt. Because he is face-to-face with his stepfather, who is calm and collected (although he is clearly worried about the bike), and who is not threatening or challenging him, Roberto is less likely to react impulsively himself and more likely to feel some responsibility to do something about the problem. It is now up to him to respond. A head-on collision has been averted and the door is open to resolve this issue.

Tyson's television

What about very young children who have limited understanding of language? How can you give a clear message to a three-year-old? When Tyson's mother saw what he was doing, she STOPPED herself from her first impulse to plead with him and put him down in a 'You' message. She saw what was happening (Step 1). She went over to him, grasped his shoulders so that he faced her, and knelt down to gain eye contact. She spoke calmly but firmly about her feelings (Step 2).

> *'I feel sad when I can't see TV.'*

As she spoke, she firmly moved him away from the TV. By pairing clear physical directions and gestures with clear speech, this youngster is more likely to understand the problem even if he doesn't comprehend the actual words. He is also less likely to be confused by his mother's apparent feelings and behaviours.

Clara's allowance

Teenagers may not appreciate direct physical contact or intense eye contact when parents are clarifying problems and feelings for them. But parents can still express their feelings and concerns honestly to teenagers like Clara. Her father bit his lip on the 'You' message he felt like giving her when she asked for an advance on her allowance, and instead listened to what she said (Step 1). He calmly but firmly stated his feelings about the situation (Step 2).

> *'**I'm** concerned when expenses are not budgeted for and we are asked for more money.'*

This statement is much less likely to provoke an emotional retaliation from Clara than the 'You' message he might have impulsively used. Rather, it invites further explanation from her, leaving the door open for shared problem solving. She may even express her own feelings in an 'I' message.

> *'Well, **I** do feel embarrassed about asking. I know I have to budget better. But, **I'll** be really disappointed if I miss the disco.'*

This is a safe and honest way to express her feelings, just as it was for her father. Notice the difference in the respectful tone of the conversation compared with the hurtful blast of 'You' messages that could be fired from both sides. We feel more confident that this parent and child will work out their problems while they are communicating so honestly.

Helping children express feelings honestly

Often children are not able to express their feelings as clearly as Clara did. They may not be able to identify their feelings in the first place or they don't know the words to describe their feelings. They, like adults, often bottle them up inside or act them out in their behaviour instead of expressing them honestly.

Parents can help their children express their feelings more clearly. To do this, they need to listen for the feeling behind what the child is saying and doing. Then, put this feeling in a sentence using the formula, *'You feel* (state feeling) *because* (state likely reason).' This is the same formula as an 'I' message, but the parent is expressing the child's 'I' message. The feeling and possible cause is reflected back to the child for checking. Use words that communicate the same strength of feeling as the child is showing. For example, she feels a *little* sad or *rather* sad or *very* sad. You will soon be told if you are wrong.

When parents reflect back their children's apparent feelings, it does not mean that they are saying they agree with the child. In fact, they may not agree with what the child is saying or doing, but they show that they have really heard and accepted that that is the way the child feels. And what's more, they have the skills as adults to put the feeling into words. Children soon learn to use feeling words themselves and to give clear 'I' messages about their feelings if their parents show them how.

Let's see how Roberto's stepfather could help his stepson express his feelings. Imagine Roberto responded to his stepfather's expressed concern about the bike on the driveway by yelling,

> *'Why are you always picking on me? I can't do anything*
> *without you complaining. Just because I'm not your son!'*

Instead of reacting to what Roberto actually said, his father looked for the feeling behind his words and actions. He then reflected this back to Roberto, adding the likely cause of this feeling.

> *'You feel very angry because you think I pick on you.'*

Roberto is not being criticised or challenged: he is being heard and his feelings are being openly expressed. He may or may not respond at this stage. He may or may not explore his feelings further. But he is much less likely to act out these feelings negatively now that they have been expressed honestly in words.

Notice that Roberto's stepfather did not buy into the *content* of what his stepson said at this stage, particularly the comment about not being his son. When children are upset about something, they often make extreme emotional statements like

> *'You don't love me.'*
> *'You only listen to her (sister).'*
> *'You're not my real father anyway.'*
> *'I wish I was dead.'*
> *'If you really cared about me, you would...'.*

These statements tug at the heartstrings and draw parents in since they feel they must respond to these words. But they often do so impulsively and emotionally. They get upset themselves and/or spend a long time reassuring their children. Then they wonder why their children keep repeating these statements: they are sure winners for drawing parent's attention and are therefore likely to keep occurring. Such statements also distract a parent's attention from the misbehaviour of the child. Children thus learn to manipulate parents' emotions to avoid the consequences of their behaviour.

A more helpful way for parents to respond to such emotional 'heart-string pullers' is to respond to the feelings behind their words, rather than the words themselves, as Roberto's stepfather did. Then put these feelings into words for the child, for example, *'You feel really miserable'* or *'You are very upset'*. Children will feel heard and understood although their parents are not saying that they agree with what was said.

Notice that it has not been suggested at any time to ask children *why* they feel like they do or *why* they behaved like they did. Children usually respond to *why* questions with *'I don't know'* or become upset because they feel they are being interrogated and they don't have the answers. 'Whys' tend to close the door on communication. Expressing *how* they feel does not interrogate or confuse them; it opens doors for children to talk more if they wish. And they will do so when they realise that this is what you are doing as well. Everyone in the family is communicating *how* they feel to each other more honestly in 'I' messages, both positive and negative feelings. This is the road the family is learning to travel.

Your communication

Ask yourself the following questions about how you and your children express or communicate feelings. Read both questions on each line before answering.

	Yes/No		Yes/No
When my child's behaviour upsets me, do I say how I feel about the behaviour?		OR do I usually go on about my child, and not mention my feelings at all?	
Am I comfortable saying 'I feel …' to my child?		OR am I uncomfortable saying, 'I feel …' to my child?	
Do I react immediately to problem behaviour with an 'I' message?		OR do I react immediately to problem behaviour with a 'You' message?	

	Yes/No		Yes/No
Do I express my feelings about the behaviour then wait for my child to make the next move?		OR do I blame my child and then tell them what to do next?	
Is my child able to express their feelings to me honestly?		OR is my child involved in 'You' battles with me and unable to express their feelings honestly?	
Do I help my child express their feelings in words?		OR do I rarely say 'You feel …' and help my child state their feelings?	

If you answered 'yes' to items in the left column, you and your children are comfortable expressing your feelings openly. Your relationships are fundamentally healthy since they are based on open and honest communication. This also means that doors are always open in your home for working out problems quickly and painlessly.

If you answered 'yes' to items in the right column, you probably realise that you and your children are not comfortable expressing your feelings to each other. Some may be locking their feelings inside; some may be acting them out. No doubt, though, these mishandled feelings are causing the bulk of your problems with your children. They are dirtying the fuel-line. They will continue to block your progress towards better relationships and better management of their behaviour.

Summary: How to express feelings at Step 2

Remember the red light is still on. STOP yourself from rushing into problems at Step 1 and STOP yourself from blaming your child in a 'You' message at Step 2. Instead:

- Decide what you are feeling about the problem.

- Approach your child face to face. With younger children, use physical cues to gain attention, for example, by placing a hand on the shoulder.

- State the feeling and the problem clearly in words using the formula,
  'I feel ... because ...'
  Use words that convey the same strength of feeling you feel (e.g. a little, quite, very annoyed) and appropriate facial expressions.

- If relevant, also reflect your child's feelings:
  'You feel (seem) ... because ...'
  stating the likely cause of the feeling if you think you know.

- Wait for your child to respond.

- If you are ignored, give an 'I' message:
  'I feel disappointed when I am ignored.'
  Again, wait for a response.

- If the child makes a move to resolve the issue, show your appreciation:
  'I really appreciate this mess being cleared up. Thank you.'

- If the child makes no response and there is still a problem, move on to the THINK steps in the next section.

Practice

To make sure that you are aware of the difference between the right way and the wrong way to express your feelings, try the exercises for Step 2 in Appendix 1

Moving on to THINK

For learners, the STOP stage is the hardest to master. As discussed before, stopping goes against our natural impulses and old attitudes about how parents should behave. In many instances, though, these STOP steps may be enough to resolve the problem, without parents actually having to do anything more about it. This is likely to be the case in families where parents and children are accustomed to communicating openly about their feelings. They will want to, and, indeed, feel they must respond to each other's 'I' messages to ease each other's stress.

The STOP steps are not likely to be enough in families where communication is generally closed and negative, where parents and children treat each other as less than friends. In times of conflict, when these parents give 'I' messages to their children, they are likely to say, *'So what!'*. Why should they help their parents feel better? If you get this response initially when you use 'I' messages with your children, be patient and try again when the next problem arises. In between problems, use 'I' messages to express your feelings about many things and help your children express their feelings about many things. In this way, you will open up the communication in your family that will make it easier to use STOP THINK DO when problems arise.

In deciding whether to move on to the THINK stage, parents also need to consider the seriousness of the behaviour or problem. Most children's misbehaviour is frustrating, annoying or irritating but not going to have earth-shattering consequences. In such milder cases, rather than moving on to THINK to discuss possible solutions with the child, parents just state their feeling about the problem, and then leave it for the child to resolve themselves. They can check back later. For example, they may say to the child *'I feel sad with that kind of talk'* or *'That behaviour really annoys me'* and then leave the child's presence. Briefly clarifying the feeling and the problem for the child while also withdrawing parental attention from the child who is mildly misbehaving may be enough to encourage more positive behaviour. Parents can then give the child positive feedback later for solving the issue.

But if the problem is not resolved or even escalates, parents move on to the THINK steps. The yellow light is on, a cue to get your brains into gear to find answers to solve the problem.

On the road, the yellow light is the driver's signal to consider which direction to take, and to get ready to go ahead. It is also the cue for the THINK stage of behaviour management. Here you prepare yourself before you actually do anything by considering your options: which road to take – and the possible consequences.

After the STOP steps, there are two steps at THINK:

- Step 3 is to THINK of solutions.
- Step 4 is to THINK about consequences.

Step 3: THINK of solutions

When situations are urgent and emotions run high, people impatiently rush through red and yellow lights in their haste to get going on green. Accidents are inevitable. Similarly, when parents have problems with their children, they often jump right over STOP and THINK, and rush headlong to DO something about them. Their impulses move them from feeling straight to doing, with very little thinking in the middle. The examples in Steps 1 and 2 showed us the damage this can cause.

STOP THINK DO suggests that if you still have a problem with your child's behaviour after you have tried the STOP steps, try some THINKING. This does not mean that you alone do the thinking: you share it with your child. This may be a new road for both of you. Because parents tend to jump in with answers, children often do not have a say about what to do to solve problems. And they often do not feel much commitment to do as they are told in this undemocratic way. They may not comply at all, or only half-heartedly, or only when their parents reach yelling or smacking point. By sharing the thinking with your children, you may actually guarantee their co-operation, or at least greatly improve the odds. In other words, your children are more likely to change their behaviour at DO if they have had a say at THINK.

Brainstorming solutions

Brainstorming refers to the process of thinking up as many answers as possible to solve a problem and it is critical at THINK. All ideas should be considered, the more the better. People are more likely to reach some agreement on what to DO if there are a number of possibilities to THINK about and choose from. Some suggestions might sound quite ridiculous or impossible when first mentioned. This doesn't matter at this stage. The important thing is that parents and children are learning and practising *how* to think, not what to think. Parents often focus on what children should think and do, and not on teaching children how to think as a process. Adults also can benefit from practice in brainstorming. They are often 'fresh out of ideas' on how to handle children and just resort to their old habitual ways. Brainstorming opens up new ways of looking at old and new problems, and is useful in many of life's situations where people have to make decisions and wear the consequences.

In real life, parents won't have time to consider all possible options for every problem that arises in the family. However, it is important to practice brainstorming initially with your children so they get the idea that there are millions of answers to problems, and thinking is the way to find them. A rule of thumb should be that parents and children consider *at least two* possibilities for resolving any issue. If the situation is urgent and quick decisions need to be made, the issue may be raised later to consider other possibilities.

Brains solve problems

Let's return to the familiar examples to brainstorm possible solutions. The suggestions listed are only the beginning. For practice in brainstorming, add to the lists yourself.

Susan's shoes

Rather than taking over the problem of getting to the dentist and rushing in to solve it herself, Susan's mother STOPS (Step 1) and expresses her feelings about the problem using an 'I' message (Step 2). Then she moves on to THINK of solutions with Susan (Step 3). Mother asks Susan to share the thinking with her:

'Susan, what can we think of to try to solve this problem?'

Susan's ideas:

> *'You can find my shoes, Mum.'*
Or   *'Let's miss the dentist.'*
Or   *'I'll wear my sandals instead.'*

Mother's ideas:

> *'I could telephone the dentist to explain.'*
Or   *'Go without your shoes.'*
Or   *'If we're late for the dentist, you'll be late for your friend's party.'*

If other members of the family are affected by this issue (eg, Susan's brother also has an appointment), they may be invited to brainstorm as well. All ideas are accepted without ridicule or judgement at this stage. What ideas have you thought of? Remember, there are probably a million answers to this problem, so open up the throttle on your mind.

Roberto's bike

Roberto's stepfather stopped himself from reacting impulsively to Roberto when he left his bike in the driveway (Step 1) and expressed his feelings and concerns to Roberto in an 'I' message (Step 2). Then he moved on to THINK of options with his son about how they could solve this issue (Step 3). He asked Roberto:

> 'What could we try to solve this problem?'

Roberto's ideas:

> *'If you're worried about it, you put the bike away.'*
Or   *'I'll put the bike away after I've had a drink.'*

Father's ideas:

> *'We could leave the bike on the driveway.'*
Or   *'Your bike will stay in the shed for a week if it is not put away now.'*

Or   *'We'll work out reminders for you to put your bike away.'*

If other children in the family leave their bikes on the driveway, they may be included in this exercise, thereby encouraging their co-operation with the outcome. What ideas have you come up with?

Tyson's television

Tyson did not respond positively to his mother's controlled (Step 1) 'I' message about how she felt when she could not see her television program (Step 2), or the non-verbal cue of moving him firmly away from the TV. He continued to stand in front of the set. His mother then moved to the THINK stage to manage this problem. While Tyson is too young to actively brainstorm solutions himself, his mother can model the process, involving him as much as possible (Step 3). This is done through the use of gesture and demonstration as she offers possible solutions for the problem.

Mother's ideas:
        'You could sit next to me and watch TV too.'
Or   *'Tyson plays in the lounge room.'*

Tyson's involvement:
        As mother says her first option, she places a chair next to
        her and seats Tyson on it.
        As she says the next option, she takes Tyson into the
        lounge room near the blocks, and leaves.

While she is thinking, mother may even consider other options like videotaping the program and playing with Tyson instead, as I am sure you have! The point is that she is THINKING and that Tyson is participating in this thinking process. His role will become more active as he gets older and more verbal. For the time being, his mother is a model for calm, controlled thinking rather than rash, emotional behaviour. A three-year-old is less likely to use tantrums to get his way if his mother doesn't use tantrums to get hers!

Clara's allowance

Recall that Clara's father is concerned about his daughter's request for money. However, by forcing his views on her and telling her what to do, he will most likely close the door on her co-operation, a scene repeated daily in families with teenagers. Instead, Clara's father STOPS himself from behaving this way (Step 1) and follows up his honest 'I' message about his concerns (Step 2) with a request for her to THINK of possible solutions to this problem with him (Step 3). He asks:

'How can we fix this problem?'

Clara's ideas:
> *'You lend me the money and I'll pay you back next week.'*

Or
> *'I could sneak in the back door of the disco like others do.'*

Parent's ideas:
> *'Why not earn some extra money this week?'*

Or
> *'You could miss the disco and we'll help you plan your budget for the next one.'*

The more ideas offered by Clara and her parents, the greater the likelihood of finding a solution that is acceptable to them all at the DO stage. You probably feel quite exhausted after thinking of your long list of possible solutions to this problem. Isn't it much easier to do when it is not your child?

Deeper thinking

Apart from solutions for specific problems, much can be learned from brainstorming about what motivates children's behaviour generally. The sorts of solutions they mostly offer, their 'pet' solutions, reflect their goals in life, what they want to happen. Children with different personalities suggest different solutions. For example, dependent children usually suggest options that 'pull others in' to their service or get them more attention. Power personalities tend to suggest options where they 'push others away' so they have control, the last say. By observing their children's suggestions, parents learn to understand their children better and how they as parents may inadvertently be reinforcing their children's immaturities, negative personality habits and problem behaviours.

Let's look at Susan and her mother again as an example of the deeper understanding that may be gained about the personalities and motives of children (and parents) by the solutions they offer. When mother asked Susan what they could do about the problem of keeping their dentist appointment, imagine she answered:

> *'Why don't you look for my shoes, Mum? You always find things.'*

Later that week, it was sports day at school and Susan left her sports clothes at home. She received a note in her diary from her teacher. When mother asked Susan what she could do about that problem, she sobbed:

> *'It's all your fault! You should put my clothes in my bag so I don't get into trouble.'*

After a few similar incidents, Susan's mother, who is learning to observe carefully and think clearly, realised that the main goal or motivation behind Susan's behaviour is to remain dependent and to draw her mother into her service. By becoming aware of this, she is in a better position to stop herself from unwittingly encouraging this immature habit in Susan. Mother also learned something about herself. She noticed that she usually came up with solutions like:

> *'I'll ring the dentist and explain'.*
> Or   *'I could write a note to your teacher to say I forgot it*
> *was sports day.'*

Her primary aim or goal seems to be to protect her daughter and be a 'good mother'. In significant ways, mother's behaviour is rein- forcing Susan's problem behaviour. By taking responsibility for Susan, mother routinely encourages her dependency. As she becomes aware of her own and her daughter's goals and realises that they are not doing Susan (or herself) any good in the longer term, mother may stop 'doing' for Susan and encourage her to 'do' for herself. These new goals of her mother's will, no doubt, be confusing and initially upset- ting for Susan. Collisions are almost unavoidable until Susan sees the benefits of taking more responsibility herself and adjusts her goals; or mother gives up in frustration. With STOP THINK DO in place, however, the latter is less likely.

As you become more aware of what your children want, what is driving their behaviour through the sorts of solutions they suggest at the THINK stage, you can bring these goals out in the open and discuss them with your children, especially older children and ado- lescents. This develops an appreciation of the individual differences between family members and an understanding of the conflicts caused when personal goals (like personalities) clash. However, while you are trying to manage problems is not the time for these discus- sions; they may be postponed until later when you are all more relaxed.

Through discussions about goals, children learn to understand themselves. Self-awareness is a good start to self-control. The same applies for parents. STOP THINK DO can thus be extended from a way of handling specific problem situations to a way of under- standing and relating more broadly and deeply with your children. A destination to look forward to on the long parenting journey!

Your solutions

Think of a problem you had recently with your child. Ask yourself the following questions about the way you handled the situation. Read both questions on each line before answering.

	Yes/No		Yes/No
Were there several answers and several ways of solving the problem?		OR was there only one right answer and one way of solving the problem?	
Did my child come up with the answer?		OR did I come up with the answer?	
Did I listen to my child's ideas without criticising them?		OR was I quick to criticise my child's ideas?	
Do I generally encourage my child to think for themselves?		OR do I generally tell my child what to think and do?	
Do I know the goals that drive my child's behaviour?		OR do I have no idea of my child's goals?	
Have I learnt what goals drive my own behaviour and affect the way I manage my child?		OR have I learnt nothing about my goals and how they affect my child's behaviour?	

If you answered 'yes' to items in the left column, you are already developing your child's THINKING skills and are probably able to think openly and broadly yourself. If you answered 'yes' to items in the right column, you are not encouraging your child to think more broadly for him or herself, but rather to think what you think. Perhaps you are also limited to a few habitual ways of handling problems with your child and need to expand your own thinking skills to include a variety of options. Like all skills that children copy from us, they will use their brains and be clever if they see their parents doing likewise.

Summary: How to think of solutions at Step 3

If your child does not respond positively to the STOP steps, remember the yellow traffic light and THINK about which direction to take to solve the problem.

- Facing your child, say:
  'Let's think of ways to solve this problem.'

- Listen attentively to your child's ideas.

- Respond pleasantly:
  'Good thinking, that is one thing we (you, I) could do. What else could we try?'

- Do not criticise, ridicule or judge any suggestion; praise their clever brains.

- Offer your own ideas as alternative possibilities:
  'OR, we (you, I) could ...'

- Encourage as many solutions as possible, and always more than one. Write suggestions down if time permits.

- If the situation is urgent and quick decisions need to be made, raise the issue later to consider other possibilities.

- Once several ideas have been generated, move on to Step 4 – THINK about the likely consequences of each suggestion.

Practice

To practice brainstorming solutions, ask your children and partner to join you in the exercise for Step 3 in Appendix 1. You will probably be surprised how good your children are at it: children are usually more divergent thinkers than adults.

Step 4: THINK about consequences

Brainstorming is like reading a map of alternative routes to reach a destination. How will you decide which road to take? It is common-sense to first consider what is likely to happen if you took each road, and how people would feel if this happened. Similarly, the solutions suggested at Step 3 are judged on the basis of likely consequences discussed rationally by those involved. They are not judged on the whims or fancies of any one person.

There are two ways of discussing likely consequences. You can brainstorm several solutions first (Step 3), and then start at the top of the list to consider each suggestion in terms of likely consequences (Step 4). You will then have a list of possible consequences as well as options. Older children cope with this method. It is also useful if a number of people are involved since it encourages a long list of alternatives for consideration before people start to evaluate consequences. Younger children may have difficulty retaining a long list of possibilities and consequences. An alternative method is to discuss the consequences of a suggestion immediately after it is made, before asking for another suggestion. Give each model a trial run in your family and then decide.

Brainstorming consequences

To practice the skill of consequential thinking, recall Susan's shoes and the various solutions discussed by Susan and her mother (Step 3). Then, take each option and brainstorm the likely consequences of that option, and how Susan and her mother would feel if this consequence happened (Step 4). This example will be discussed in detail to clarify the thinking process, although it is not expected that you will explore consequences so fully in real-life situations.

Susan's mother restates each suggestion that they thought of in Step 3 and then asks her daughter:

> *'What might happen if we tried that suggestion?*
> *How would we feel if this consequence happened?'*

Mother may need to offer lots of her own ideas about consequences in the beginning.

Suggestion 1:   *'You find my shoes, Mum.'*

Consequence a:	Mother may be late getting ready herself.
Feelings:	Mother is annoyed; Susan doesn't care.
Consequence b:	Susan is reinforced for behaving immaturely.
Feelings:	Mother is concerned; Susan doesn't care.
Consequence c:	Mother finds shoes and attends the dentist.
Feelings:	Mother has short-term relief; Susan is pleased.

Suggestion 2:   *'Let's miss the dentist.'*

Consequence a:	Susan's toothache does not get attention.
Feelings:	Mother feels guilty; Susan is hurting.
Consequence b:	The dentist will still charge for the appointment.
Feelings:	Mother is annoyed; Susan feels guilty.

Suggestion 3:   *'I'll wear my sandals instead.'*

Consequence a:	They make the appointment on time.
Feelings:	Both are pleased.

Consequence b: Shoes still need to be found later.
Feelings: Mother annoyed; Susan doesn't care.

Suggestion 4: *'I could telephone the dentist to explain.'*

Consequence a: Courteous to dentist but doesn't solve problem.
Feelings: Mother still frustrated; Susan relieved.

Consequence b: Susan learns that her mother will save her.
Feelings: Mother is worried; Susan is happy.

Suggestion 5: *'Go without your shoes.'*

Consequence a: Appointment made on time.
Feelings: Mother is relieved; Susan is embarrassed.

Consequence b: Shoes still need to be found later.
Feelings: Mother annoyed; Susan doesn't care.

Suggestion 6: *'If we're late for the dentist, you'll be late for your friend's party'*

Consequence a: Susan gets very upset and wastes more time.
Feelings: Mother is still exasperated; Susan is more upset.

Consequence b: Susan finds shoes and appointment is kept.
Feelings: Mother is pleased; Susan feels resentful.

Consequence c: Mother does not carry out her threat.
Feelings: Mother feels defeated; Susan is relieved.

While this process seems lengthy, it is important to allow time in the initial stages of learning to practise brainstorming and thinking about consequences to demonstrate that there are millions of answers and millions of consequences that can be considered for any one problem. This opens up new possibilities for handling problems for parents and children. Remember also that children are more likely to carry out the chosen solution at DO if they are involved beforehand in considering that solution and its likely consequences, along with all the others offered at THINK. With practice, shortcuts will be found for handling more urgent situations.

For more practice in consequential thinking, consider the various solutions offered for Roberto's Bike, Tyson's Television and Clara's Allowance at Step 3. Follow the format for Susan's Shoes above to THINK about at least one likely consequence for each solution offered and also, how those involved might feel about these consequences.

Summary: How to think about consequences at Step 4

The yellow light is switched on, and so are your brains. You have thought of possible options to solve the problem (Step 3), and now you THINK about likely consequences of these options (Step 4)

- State a suggested solution to your child. Then ask:

  'What might happen if we (you, I), tried that?'

- Listen attentively to suggested consequences.

- Offer your own ideas about likely consequences.

- After the consequence is suggested, ask your child:

  'How would you feel if that happened?'

  or put your child's apparent feelings into words, eg,

  'I can see that you would not be happy about that.'

- Express your own feelings about the consequence in an 'I' message.

- Move on with your child to choose the best option at DO.

Practice

Ask your children and partner to join you again at Step 4 in Appendix 1 to consider the consequences of the suggestions made in the previous exercise. Praise their good brains.

Moving on to DO

Now that you have considered the different roads to your destination of solving the problem with your child, you are ready to choose one road and go ahead on it. Because you have considered the likely consequences, you are more assured of making a good choice. The yellow light is changing to green and you can move on to a solution that is likely to work at DO.

On the road, the green light signals the driver to go, to move ahead towards a chosen direction. The green light is also the cue for DO when you finally act to solve the problem you are having with your child's behaviour.

After the STOP and THINK steps, there are two steps at DO:

- Step 5 is to choose the best solution to DO.
- Step 6 is to DO it, to put it into action.

Step 5: Choose a solution

Needless to say, children need a say in choosing what to DO at Step 5. If they are invited to offer ideas at THINK but not included in the final choice of what to DO, they will feel cheated of their rights in this democratic process, and their parents will be cheated of their rights to responsible behaviour and co-operation from their children. When people have an active role in making choices and decisions, they feel respected, and are also respectful of those who give them these rights. Plus, they feel more committed to doing what they said they would do.

Decisions and choices

In reality, however, many parents are not really comfortable allowing their children to make their own choices and decisions. Maybe they have the old, ingrained attitude that parents know what is best for their children. Or maybe they doubt whether their children are capable themselves. Or maybe they just don't want their beloved children to make mistakes and experience pain if they can help them avoid it. Whatever the motives behind their reluctance to allow their children to make decisions, their children will pick up the message as a vote of 'no confidence' from their parents: they will feel their parents don't believe they can do it. The fact is that children only become confident and capable by having a go themselves – by actually making decisions and choices in matters that affect them and by making some mistakes. As we all do, our children will learn from the consequences of their choices, and will make better choices next time – the same way they will learn to drive a car.

Here's a tip for developing decision-making skills in your children ... Give them lots of choices in everyday matters (like egg or cereal for breakfast, jeans or black pants to wear, a movie or the circus for a family visit). When they make a choice, however, generally follow through with their decision, even if they change their mind. Making choices means standing by them and seeing them through. You are preparing them for the 'big' decisions in life when you won't always be around to steer them along the way or save them in the end.

Choosing the best solution

When solving particular problems using STOP THINK DO, choosing the best solution at DO (Step 5) means choosing the option proposed at THINK that has the most acceptable consequences for the people involved. Because several possible solutions have been discussed openly in terms of their consequences and how people would feel if these happened, it may not be difficult to make a choice between them at Step 5. Especially in the early stages of learning STOP THINK DO, it is important that parents give their children votes of confidence by often agreeing to try their child's choices if they are reasonable, even if parents are not convinced that they are the best solutions. Children will learn from the experience for next time. Parents may even be surprised at what can work if their children are committed to it.

If parents and children cannot agree on one best solution, a compromise needs to be negotiated that combines some options or amends others. It is essential to reach *some* agreement on a plan of action so those involved are committed to make the plan work. If several people are involved, full agreement may not be possible anyway, and a majority vote may be taken. However, a review time (an hour, day or week later to suit the issue) should always be set so that progress may be checked and changes made to ensure that the process is not seen to fail.

Indeed, there is no failure in STOP THINK DO. If a solution

isn't working out well, it is just another opportunity for more thinking and decision making because there are millions of possible solutions for each problem. Answers will always be found if parents and children are talking, thinking and planning together. Remember, you are all driving for the same team.

Consider how the people in our familiar examples might finally choose what to DO to solve their problems.

Susan's shoes

Susan and her mother thought of 6 possible solutions to their problem of getting to the dentist (Step 3), and discussed some likely consequences of each option (Step 4). In their discussions, they eliminated some ideas because they were not happy about what might happen if they tried them. They were left with a few ideas that seemed acceptable. Susan's mother asked her daughter for her opinion about which of these she would choose to DO (Step 5) by saying:

'Which do you think is the best to choose?'

Susan's choice:
'I think you should ring the dentist and ask him if we can be a little late. That will give us enough time to look for my shoes.'

Mother then gave her own choice:
'Well, I really like your idea of wearing your sandals now. You could look for your shoes later.'

They discussed these choices to reach a compromise.
Compromise choice:
Mother telephones the dentist out of courtesy to say they will be a little late while Susan puts on her sandals.

This is the plan Susan and her mother decided to put into action.

Roberto's bike

At THINK, Roberto and his stepfather discussed several possible solutions to the problem of his bike on the driveway (Step 3) and their likely consequences (Step 4). It was now time to choose one solution to DO (Step 5). Father asked Roberto:

'Which solution do you think is best?'

Roberto's choice:
  'I'll have a drink at the tap outside as I'm putting my bike away.'

In fact, Roberto has offered a compromise of his need to have a drink and the need to move his bike. Children are quite skilled at compromise, providing they see the reason for it and are allowed the opportunity.

Father then gave his choice:
  'That seems okay by me.'
They have agreed on a plan of action.

Tyson's television

Very young children are not capable of too much verbal negotiation. How can they be involved in making decisions and choices? Tyson's mother showed him through gesture and simple words the solutions that she considered were possible (Step 3). She showed him the consequences of each (Step 4). Which one would they choose to DO (Step 5)?

Tyson's choice:
  He expressed his choice through his behaviour. After his mother demonstrated the possibilities, he returned to sit on the chair next to her.

Mother's choice:
  She lifted him on the chair and continued to watch her program with him.

Mother and Tyson have agreed on a plan of action.

Clara's allowance

The tone of voice parents use and their facial expressions are very important when they are discussing choices and negotiating compromises with their children. People remain respectful and positive throughout the process. This is particularly true when teenagers are involved. They tend to be super-sensitive about being spoken to like a child or like a criminal. Having discussed possible solutions to the problem of money for the disco with his daughter (Step 3) and eliminating some because they were not happy about the likely consequences (Step 4), Clara's father now suggested she make a choice about what to DO (Step 5). He asked:

'What do you think is the best option?'

Clara's choice:
> *'If you lend me the money for the disco this week, I'll do extra work on the weekend when I don't have so much homework.'*

Father then gave his choice:
> *'Since this may come up again, I would like you to set aside time on the weekend to discuss your budget.'*

Mother may also give her choice. The tone of the discussion is right for Clara and her parents to come to some agreement. They keep talking.

Compromise choice:
> Parents agreed to lend Clara money. She agreed to work for it on the weekend and to discuss her budget on Saturday morning.

A plan of action has been chosen. The outlook is optimistic. Relationships are running smoothly.

Your choices

Think about the way choices and decisions are made in your family. Consider the following, reading both questions on each line before answering.

Yes/No		Yes/No	
Do I often ask my child's opinions about things?		OR do I rarely ask my child's opinions?	
Do I often give my child choices?		OR do I rarely give my child choices?	
Do I have confidence in my child's ability to make decisions?		OR do I not have confidence in my child's ability to make decisions?	
Do I negotiate and compromise with my child?		OR do I insist on 'What I say goes'?	
Do I accept that my child can't do things as well as I can, but will learn with encouragement?		OR do I believe that if my child can't do things as well as I can, they are a failure and need my help?	

If you answered 'yes' to questions in the left column, you are encouraging your children to think for themselves and allowing them the freedom to make their own decisions and choices about what to do. They will feel confident in themselves because you have confidence in them. If you answered 'yes' to items in the right column, you seem to believe that you alone should make decisions for your children. Maybe you feel that you know best or that your children aren't capable themselves or you just don't want them to make mistakes. Whichever way, they will be picking up this 'no confidence' message from you. Confidence is only gained by having a go.

Summary: How to choose a solution at Step 5

After you STOP and THINK about options for solving the problem and their consequences, the green light is on. Time to DO something – move towards a particular direction or choice of action to solve the problem

- Ask your child:
  'What do you think is the best solution?'

- Listen attentively.

- State your own choice of solutions.

- As often as possible, agree to try your child's choice if it is reasonable. You are giving them a vote of confidence.

- If you and your child agree on what to try, DO it (Step 6).

- If you don't agree, suggest a compromise or ask your child to suggest one. Negotiate until an agreement is reached that you are both willing to try at Step 6.

- Stay calm. Keep your tone of voice and facial expression positive. You are teaching your child the skills of decision making, compromise and negotiation.

- Set a review time to check progress and make changes if necessary, before people feel the process has failed – there are simply more options to consider.

Practice

See if the members of your family can agree on a solution to the practice exercise at Step 5 in Appendix 1.

Step 6: Act!

Now you're on the chosen path, go for it! To put the chosen plan into action, you or your child, or both, will probably need to do or say something that will resolve the conflict. But what if your child can't do the chosen action? Sometimes, children do not have the ability required: they may be young or unskilled or inexperienced. In such instances, parents break the action into smaller steps and guide their children through these steps according to their ability and maturity.

Training skills at DO

Consider Jed, who tipped orange juice over the floor while pouring a drink for his friend, Mai. His father followed the STOP THINK DO steps below to manage the problem effectively.

STOP

Step 1:

 Father STOPPED himself from his first impulse to smack or berate his son.

 Instead, he looked at what had happened.

Step 2:

 He STOPPED himself from blaming his son in a 'You' message like:

  'Can't you do anything without making a mess!'

 Instead, he expressed his feelings about the problem:

  'I feel really annoyed when I walk on sticky floors.'

THINK

Step 3:

 He asked his son to THINK of ways of solving this problem. Jed and he suggested options like:

  Mother wipes the floor (!).

The drink was for Mai, so she can clean it up.

Jed cleans up the mess.

Step 4:

They discussed some consequences of these options, like:

Mother is too busy and wouldn't like the idea of cleaning up anyway.

Mai might want to go home if she is asked to clean up.

Jed won't do a good job of cleaning up.

DO

Step 5:

They agreed on a solution to DO:

Father helps Jed to wipe up the juice before he plays with Mai.

Step 6:

They put the plan into action. Father broke the action into four smaller steps:

bring the cloth from the laundry

wipe the floor

squeeze the cloth out

rinse the cloth in the sink.

Since Jed was hesitant to begin, father demonstrated the skills required, which his son then copied. His father also encouraged each step and acknowledged his son's efforts to learn the task, even if the job was not done perfectly. As he practises these steps in similar situations, he will become more skilled.

As discussed in the first chapter, children are learners in everything. They cannot do things as well as adults can. They will learn as long as they are encouraged. This is an important point to keep in mind at DO when managing a problem with your child – the action decided upon may need to be broken into smaller steps with you demonstrating some steps for your child to imitate, and with you encouraging their efforts. Encouragement is the fuel for your children's confidence and competence.

Following up

If you reached your destination, the plan of action worked and the problem is solved, congratulations! Make sure you follow up this success: discuss with your children, your partner or friends how STOP THINK DO worked for that problem. This encourages everyone – including sceptics – to try it for more problems.

You can even use this success as a licence to drive further. This is what Susan's mother did. Recall that she and her daughter had agreed that Susan would put on her sandals while mother rang the dentist to say they would be a little late. This was their chosen solution to the problem (Step 5). They put this plan into action (Step 6) and it worked quite well. On her return from the dentist, mother followed up the success by commenting on how well the plan did work. Susan was pleased and proud; mother was relieved and reassured. So she moved a little further. She raised the issue of the missing shoes with Susan. Since the pressure of keeping the appointment had now gone, she had time to guide Susan through the STOP THINK DO steps again to come up with answers about how to find her shoes. Then she went even further. She extended the discussion to how Susan could keep track of her shoes (and other possessions) so that she can find them quickly next time.

In this way, mother encouraged her daughter to take more responsibility for herself and her belongings, without ever putting her down or becoming distressed herself. Because mother spoke to Susan in a respectful way and because she encouraged her co-operation with a specific problem like the dentist appointment, Susan is likely to co-operate further with other issues related to responsibility and independence. Mother used a specific success as encouragement for Susan to develop as a whole person and outgrow her immature, dependent habits.

Similarly, Clara's father now had a licence to drive further with his daughter. Recall how her parents agreed to lend her the money for the disco and she would repay them with chores on the weekend, and also discuss her budget (Step 5). They put this plan into action

(Step 6) and it worked reasonably well. All parties were pleased. Father built on this success by arranging with Clara a set time on Saturday morning for extending the discussion from the specific problem of money for the disco to the broader issues of budgeting and financial responsibility. There is also a good chance that father will learn more about his daughter's habits and friends – to ease his concerns – through this positive talk and shared planning session. And this, without any put downs, punishments or price to pay!

In fact, responsibility, independence, maturity, self-confidence, self-esteem, self-control, respect for others – all the things we want our children to develop – are only the sum total of lots of specific successes like Susan had with her shoes, Roberto with his bike and Clara with her allowance. And, handling such specific situations well is the best parents can do to prepare their children for happy and responsible adulthood and also to strengthen their own relationships with their children. All the better if they start at Tyson's age!

Contingency plans

Even when we are on the road heading towards our destination, it is a good idea to have contingency plans in case something goes wrong. What if the plan of action you negotiated with your children does not work for long and the same problem occurs again later? Sometimes the situation is a little different with other people involved, or it occurs in another place where the same solution might not fit. If this happens, treat it as a new problem, STOP and work through THINK and DO steps again to find another answer. There are always more answers – you and your children just have to keep thinking. With more practice, shortcuts will be found, and the process will become quick, natural and automatic.

Sometimes, the problem is not even resolved initially since the child may not DO at Step 6 what they agreed to DO when the solution was chosen at Step 5. They may have been distracted from the action, or may not have felt committed enough to follow through, or may only have partially completed the action. How do parents handle this situation? They could go back through the STOP THINK DO steps again with the child and decide on another option to do as mentioned above. This can be time consuming. Alternatively, they can shortcut the process by giving the child another choice: the child does as was agreed at Step 5 or something else, with the 'something else' being another option that was discussed at the THINK stage but not chosen at DO. It is a consequence of not doing the chosen solution properly and is likely to be less attractive to the child otherwise it would have been chosen at Step 5. Some examples will make this clearer. Imagine that the children in our familiar situations did not put into action the plan they agreed to in Step 5, and that the problems were still unresolved.

Susan's shoes

Chosen solution at Step 5:

> Mother telephones dentist while Susan puts on sandals.

Action taken:

> Mother telephones dentist. Susan watches TV and forgets sandals.

Mother's contingency plan – offer Susan the following choice:

> *'You may put on your sandals as agreed*
> *or you may go to the dentist without any shoes.'*

'Going without shoes' was one of the solutions suggested at the THINK stage. The consequences of this suggestion were discussed by Susan and her mother. It was not Susan's choice at the time, but she now has the choice again. Or she may choose to put on her sandals as she originally agreed and the problem is resolved. It is up to her. If she puts her sandals on, mother expresses her appreciation in an 'I' message.

> *'I appreciate your help in getting ready. Thank you.'*

If Susan does not put on her sandals, mother may assume, quite logically, that she has chosen the other alternative, namely, not to wear
any shoes ... and may take her barefooted to the dentist. Mother
explains this calmly in a non-critical, matter-of-fact way. When she
is ready to leave, she approaches Susan and says:

> *'Since you don't have your sandals on,*
> *you have chosen to go without any shoes to the dentist.'*

Mother *must* be prepared to follow through with this consequence if
this method is to work. No more words, just action from this point.
Mother takes Susan barefooted to the dentist. She remains positive but
firm, in control of herself and the situation. She does not react emotionally or make value judgments about her daughter; she does not yell
or threaten or blame or put Susan down. She simply carries through
with her daughter's choice of action. The focus is not the child, but the
behaviour that is the child's choice and responsibility. And the relationship between mother and daughter is not jeopardised.

   It is important to add encouragement for future situations.
Susan's mother assures her daughter that she will have a chance to
choose differently on another day. When a similar problem arises in
the future, Susan will know that she can choose the outcome and prevent consequences that she does not like. She is also aware that her
mother will follow through with these consequences if necessary. It
is, again, up to Susan.

Roberto's bike

Chosen solution at Step 5:
   Roberto gets drink from tap as he puts bike away.
Action taken:
   Roberto has drink but goes off to play, forgetting bike.
Father's contingency plan – offer Roberto the following choice:
   'You may put your bike away now or it will be in the shed for a
   week.'

The option of the bike being put in the shed was discussed at THINK, but not chosen at DO. If Roberto now chooses not to put his bike away as he had agreed, it is logical to conclude that he is not concerned about his bike, and has chosen to be without it for a week. If he puts his bike away, his father expresses his appreciation. If he doesn't, his stepfather tells his son:

> *'Since you chose not to put your bike away as we agreed,*
> *you have chosen to be without your bike for a week'.*

Father then acts with no more discussion. While he is putting the bike in the shed, he lets Roberto know that he will have a chance to make another choice next week: he may then choose to behave responsibly with his bike. Father uses a firm but friendly tone of voice and manner that preserves his relationship with his stepson, solves the immediate problem and encourages Roberto to behave more responsibly in future.

Note that this situation is quite different from one in which the parent imposes his own will on his child. Roberto had a say all the way. He suggested solutions and discussed consequences, including those of being without his bike for a week. He chose what to DO along with his stepfather at Step 5. These factors should have ensured his commitment to the action plan. When he did not comply at Step 6 for some reason (eg, he forgot and went to play), he again had a choice to comply or experience the consequences of not complying. Roberto is behind the wheel.

Tyson's television

Chosen solution at Step 5:
> Tyson sits near mother to watch television with her.

Action taken:
> Tyson watches the program for a while. He then becomes restless and puts his hands over mother's eyes so that she can't see TV.

Mother's contingency plan – offer Tyson this choice again:

> '*You can watch TV here with mummy* (removing Tyson's hands from her eyes) *or you can play here by yourself*' (leading him into the lounge room and pointing to blocks).

If Tyson sits nicely, she thanks him. If he continues to interrupt her program, she calmly takes him into the lounge, shuts the door and returns to her seat since he is obviously not interested in sitting with her. If he tantrums, she should not pay attention to him since he has chosen not to be with her.

As mother offers him choices in many situations throughout the day and consistently follows through with the consequences of his choices, Tyson will learn that it is largely he and not his mother who determines the outcome: he can avoid consequences he doesn't like by choosing appropriately. As well, he is learning to respect his mother's rights, as he himself is being respectfully handled.

Clara's allowance

Chosen solution at Step 5:

> Parents lend Clara money for disco. She works to repay it and discusses her budget with her parents on the weekend.

Action taken:

> Parents lend Clara money. She goes to the disco. On Saturday, she complains of being tired and having too much homework to waste time working for parents or discussing finances.

Parents' contingency plan – offer Clara this choice:

> '*You may do as you agreed before the disco*
> *or you may pay us back with your allowance next week.*'

At THINK, Clara had considered the consequences of advancing her allowance and had not chosen this solution when she remembered that she needed her allowance next week for a pair of jeans. Now, she has the choice again. If she stays in her room on Saturday morning, father could logically assume that she has chosen the option of forfeiting her allowance the following week. His next step is clear. When it is time for her to receive her next allowance, he explains to her in a firm but positive tone:

> *'Since you chose not to do as you agreed last week, you have chosen to forfeit your allowance this week. But we can discuss the budget issue more fully any time you wish.'*

Clara has the power to change the situation and avoid consequences she does not like in the future. Her parents have the power over the consequences they offer. It can be a win-win situation.

The power of consequences

Offering children choices of consequences is designed to increase their sense of responsibility to do what they say, to follow through with their commitment to resolve issues. But many parents say that they have tried using consequences with their children in the past, but they haven't worked. There are many reasons why consequences might not have worked including:

- Parents have not followed through with consequences consistently and the child doesn't believe they will.
- They offer consequences after a period of begging, pleading, yelling, nagging or smacking where the pain of the consequence does not outweigh all the attention children received prior to it.
- They were upset or angry when they offered the consequence, and then went back on it when they calmed down or when their children begged them or promised to be good.

When parents are using STOP THINK DO, the above scenarios will not apply. Parents will be calm and controlled in their manner and words, positive in their encouragement of their children to make good choices, and they will always do what they say. They will act on consequences rather than talk about them, and emotions will not cloud the issue. Moreover, because their children have been directly involved in the thinking and choosing of options and consequences, they are more likely to accept the consequence if it happens and less likely to get upset, overreact and take it personally.

However, be warned. There can still be problems, especially in the early stages of your STOP THINK DO journey. Parents do have to accept that they may lose in the short term with this method, that is, the specific problem may not be resolved at Step 6. Roberto's father could end up putting the bike away himself or Clara's father could end up out of pocket. Sometimes children ignore parents when they offer consequences, or say they don't care about the consequence, or get emotional or angry because they do care. This may occur even after they have been involved in shared problem solving with parents and have discussed the relative merits of the consequence being offered, although it will certainly decrease as the STOP THINK DO method becomes more ingrained in the family.

When children do not comply with agreed solutions and do not respond positively to the choice of consequences offered as a contingency plan, parents accept this set-back and get around the problem some way other than with their child's compliance. But they definitely must follow through with the consequence the child chose. If parents don't follow through, *they* are not doing what they say – *they* are now being irresponsible. They are showing their child that it is not necessary to listen to parents at STOP or seriously think about options and consequences at THINK or even make considered choices at DO, because their parents won't follow through with what they said anyway. Children may need to experience consequences so that they have a clear memory of what happens if they do not stop and think first, make good choices, and do what they say they would.

Family meetings

If the same problems seem to be recurring or if several members of the family are affected by a particular problem, these issues can be raised at family meetings where all the family attends for a regular time each week, for about 20 minutes. Family meetings provide continuing practice for all the family in the STOP THINK DO steps.

They should not only be about problems, however. Families can plan positive events like outings or discuss everyday matters that affect the whole family.

Family members rotate to chair the meetings, with parents demonstrating this role initially. The chairperson invites a discussion about one or two issues per meeting. Everyone who is affected by the issue states their feelings about it and their suggestions for solving it. They choose a plan of action that may require negotiation and compromise. If complete agreement cannot be reached, a majority vote is taken and everyone is encouraged to give this plan a go for the next week. The outcome is reviewed at the next family meeting. If this plan does not work, consequences for continuing problems are decided by everyone and apply equally to everyone who chooses not to comply. The atmosphere at family meetings is friendly and rational, not emotional or judgmental. Even when problems are being discussed, individuals are not threatened or blamed. They are asked for their commitment and encouraged to comply. But, it is up to them.

You are now invited to stop off at the Scotts' house and join their family meeting. Saturday morning at 9 o'clock is family meeting time. This family consists of the mother, Roberto aged 12, Kate aged 14, stepfather and his son, Sean, aged 6 years. Notice the use of 'I' messages and positive language by parents, the reflection of children's feelings, guidance through STOP THINK DO to solve problems and the negotiation of follow-up consequences.

Mother: *'I think I'm chairperson this week. Let's see how we went with our problem for last week before we look at new things.'*

Sean: *'Yuk! Do we have to do this? I'm sick of it.'*

Mother: *'You're bored, Sean, talking about things from last week.'*

Sean: *'Yeah, I want to watch cartoons.'*

Mother: *'If you want to go and watch TV you can. But remember that whatever we decide goes until the next meeting.'*

Sean: *'Oh, that's not fair!'*

Mother: *'Later we can discuss the time of this meeting if it clashes with your cartoon program. But first, let's discuss the problem of bikes left lying around.'*

Kate: *'It didn't work. Roberto dumped his bike right on my flower garden!'*

Father: *'You're annoyed about that, Kate. I was angry too when I backed the car into someone's bike yesterday.'*

Roberto: *'That was Kate's bike. See, I'm not the only one to blame!'*

Father: *'You're upset because you think you're being blamed. We are all using our brains to work out answers here, so no one is being blamed'*

Mother: *'Well, what can we do about this problem? Any ideas?'*

Sean: *'Why don't you take their bikes away?'*

Kate: *'Why don't you keep out of it, stupid?'*

Mother: *'Kate, everyone has a say at family meetings. What's your idea?'*

Kate: *'I always forget about putting my bike away when I get home. We need something to remind us.'*

Roberto: *'I know. What about painting a red light on the door of the garage? We will see it as we ride round the corner.'*

Mother: *'Good thinking, Roberto. Okay, let's look at the ideas we've got. What would happen if we tried the idea of taking the bikes away?'*

Kate: *'Well, I need mine to get to school. It's too far to walk.'*

Mother: *'So, you wouldn't be happy about that option.'*

Roberto: *'Neither would I.'*

Mother: *'What about Roberto's idea of the red light? I'm a bit concerned that the neighbours might object – you know Mrs Clarke!'*

Kate: *'I'll explain it to her first. She will probably be pleased not having bikes left against her fence.'*

Mother: *'Do we agree to give the red light a try? Let's take a vote.'* *Since this problem of bikes keeps coming up, what consequences should people have if they keep on forgetting?'*

Father: *'Maybe we could consider the suggestion of taking bikes away from those who are not behaving responsibly with them.'*

Roberto: *'The same has to happen for Sean's skateboard!'*

Mother: *'The same applies to anyone who leaves things around that could cause accidents. I'll have to watch my wheelbarrow!'*

Kate: *'I'll agree if everyone else does.'*

Roberto: *'Me too.'*

Father: *'Okay. Shall we make up the red light this afternoon?*
                We will discuss how this idea is working at our next family
                meeting.'

Sean: *'Can I help with the light?'*

Mother: *'I thought you wanted to talk about the time of our meet-*
                ings, Sean.'

Sean: *'Maybe next week – this is more fun!'*

We will leave the Scott family at this point. Hopefully you can
follow the STOP THINK DO steps in this example. One imagines
that this family could cope with anything by using the skills they
have learned and the respect they have gained for each other. The
roadway seems clear ahead.

Summary: How to act at Step 6

The green light is still on and it is time to put the chosen plans into action at DO.

- If necessary, break the action into small steps that you demonstrate and then encourage your child to try.

- When the problem is resolved, express your appreciation. Discuss successes later for further reinforcement and to motivate children to try the method again.

- If the problem recurs and circumstances are changed to some degree, treat it as a new problem and repeat STOP THINK DO steps.

- If the problem is not resolved because the child did not act on the chosen solution, you can go back to STOP and THINK again about what to DO. Or to shortcut the process, offer another choice in a calm and friendly manner.
  'You may do as you agreed
  or you may (alternative solution discussed at THINK
  that is a consequence of not complying).'

- If your child still chooses not to act as agreed, say:
  'Since you have chosen not to (chosen solution),
  I assume that you have chosen (alternative solution as
  consequence).'

- Say nothing else. Act! Follow through with consequences calmly.

- While acting, assure your child that they will have a chance to choose differently next time to avoid consequences they may not like. It is up to them.

- If problems recur frequently and involve several family members, raise the issues at regular family meeting times and negotiate plans and consequences as a group.

Practice

Try the practice exercise at Step 6 in Appendix 1 to work out contingency plans if the agreed solution did not work out. Check the list of suggestions at Step 4 to find an alternative to offer as a consequence.

Below is a summary of what to *say* and *do* to manage children's behaviour.

STOP Step 1. **STOP, look and listen**
Don't react, say nothing, observe.

Step 2. **Express feelings honestly**
'*I feel* (state feeling) *because* (state problem).'

THINK Step 3. **THINK of solutions**
'*What can we try to solve this problem?*'

Step 4. **THINK about consequences**
'*What might happen if we tried that?*'
'*How would we feel then?*'

DO Step 5. **Choose a solution**
'*What solution do we agree on?*'

Step 6. **Act!**
'*Let's try it.*' Praise efforts.
If it doesn't work, offer another choice
'*You may* (agreed solution)
or you may (alternative solution as a consequence)'
OR go back to STOP and THINK about
what to DO

After some practice in this process, shortcuts will be found as people begin to think and choose quickly like

STOP	*'I feel ... because ...'*
THINK	*'How can we solve it?'*
DO	*'Let's try it.'*
	If it doesn't work:
	'You may (agreed solution) *or you may* (consequence).'

In the next chapter, you will learn how to teach your children these steps to solve problems with others. You are their guide.

Chapter 4

TRAINING CHILDREN'S SOCIAL SKILLS

Why teach your children to drive?

In Chapter 3, parents learned how to use STOP THINK DO to manage their children's behaviour effectively. An additional benefit is that, by using this method to solve problems at home, parents are actually demonstrating or modelling good social skills for their children. They are showing their children how to behave with others, especially when they have problems to solve with them. And this *life skill* can benefit their children in all situations – at home, at school, in the work place and later, in their own families. Take an example in the schoolyard: a child is having problems with another child, but instead of reacting impulsively, often with bad habits like sulking, dobbing, yelling, hitting or panicking, this child has learned from their parent's management at home that they will have better consequences if they stop first, control their emotions and think about their options. This is what their parents do with them at home when they have problems … and it works!

Chapter 4 extends the benefits parents using STOP THINK DO can offer their children. It shows parents how to directly teach their children to use STOP THINK DO themselves to solve problems with their friends and siblings. Training children to use STOP THINK DO to improve their own social skills is like teaching *them* to drive a car. Parents need to stress the rules of the road, the importance of responsible attitudes and impulse control, and even what to do at traffic lights!

But, before parents put energy into training their children, they need to be reassured that the effort is worthwhile. I am sure all parents agree how important it is for children to be taught to drive a car skilfully, confidently and safely: their life will depend on it. Similarly, teaching children to use STOP THINK DO themselves can be a life-saving decision, at least in terms of ensuring the quality of a child's life. There are decades of research and clinical evidence that support this fact. It shows that children need good social skills to help them develop good social relationships, especially with their peers. If they don't have good social skills and relationships, they are vulnerable for serious psychological, behavioural and emotional problems in their childhood and even later in adolescence and adulthood. These problems include delinquency, criminality, drug dependence, dropping out of school, academic and employment difficulties, low self-esteem and motivation, loneliness, depression, and anxiety – all things we desperately want our children to avoid.

It is also worrying to learn from research and clinical experience that around 10 per cent of school-age children have significant social problems, even higher for children with disabilities. This means that about three children in the average classroom are at risk of serious damage to the quality of their lives. And the suffering is not only personal. Society ultimately bears the cost of providing the medical, legal and welfare support for people who are damaged by early emotional and social difficulties, just as it ultimately pays for the personal and property damage from accidents on the road.

Unfortunately, children do not always learn the social skills they need naturally, especially growing up in today's society. Today's children face enormous pressures – family breakdown, availability of drugs, rising crime rates, aggressive media, job insecurity, challenges to authority, racial and religious tension and a very fast pace of life. These pressures can interfere with children learning the skills they need, and threaten their emotional and social stability. Some children lack emotional maturity and skills themselves to handle these pressures. Others lack appropriate role models in their life to teach and demonstrate the necessary skills for them. Without protective skills, they become victims who create more victims. Consider the tragedies that have occurred throughout the world in recent years where children who are loners with poor social skills, ostracised or mistreated by their mainstream peers, take their revenge on their classmates, parents and teachers with devastating consequences. Yes, most people agree on the importance of good social skills and good social relationships on children's personal wellbeing and adjustment, and that of society generally.

Training social skills with STOP THINK DO

In response to these serious concerns for today's children, many programs for training social skills in children have been developed around the world over recent decades. The aim of many of these programs is to develop emotional–social intelligence and skills in children to improve their relationships with all people in their lives, and enable them to make and keep friends. The programs often include parents and teachers as trainers. STOP THINK DO is one such program and is supported by years of research and practice.

Some of the specific attributes and skills developed using STOP THINK DO include:

- listening skills;
- conversational skills;
- recognising and expressing feelings appropriately;
- understanding the feelings of others;
- respect for self and others;
- self-control and self-discipline;
- self-esteem and self-confidence;
- problem-solving skills;
- knowledge of appropriate social behaviour in different situations;
- logical thinking and evaluating skills;
- thinking ahead, planning skills;
- taking responsibility, making decisions and choices;
- co-operative negotiation skills; and
- behavioural skills to act appropriately.

Parents may be reassured that by teaching their children these STOP THINK DO skills following the instructions in Chapter 4, they may prevent serious and long-lasting negative effects of poor social relationships in their own children. In addition to the instructions in this chapter, there are other resources available for parents undertaking this task. They may use the *STOP and THINK Friendship* video and workbook mentioned in Appendix 3. This provides an exciting visual medium and fun format that helps parents teach their children the process and skills outlined in this chapter. It is suitable for children aged about six to 12 years. If parents wish to understand more about STOP THINK DO, including background research and development of the program and how it is applied in school class-rooms, they may refer to Appendix 3 for references including the STOP THINK DO website. Let's now move on to the social skills training steps, with some road warnings first.

Overtaking is a hazard

Parents may not like the way their children relate with other chil-dren, their friends or brothers and sisters, or how they handle problems with them. They may feel annoyed, frustrated, worried or even angry about these hassles. Their natural response may be to intervene, advise, preach, direct or tell their children how to solve their problems. Most parents admit, however, that these techniques generally don't work: their children get more upset or ignore them or return to the same hassle after a while.

In fact, overtaking can be a hazard. Parental interference often makes peer or sibling conflicts worse, as in the following situation:

> Nine-year-old Sonja was playing in her room with Kael, a child from her school. After a while, mother heard her daughter yell and saw Kael walk out of the room sulking. Mother was tired of Sonja's bossy, stubborn nature. She felt exasperated. She went to Sonja's room and blurted out these 'You' messages:

> *'Why are you behaving like this? No wonder you haven't any friends. You should apologise to Kael.'*

> Sonja began to cry and immediately went on the defensive:

> *'It's not my fault. You always blame me. Blame him!'*

She kicked the game over the floor and lunged angrily at Kael, who was sulking in the doorway. He ran out of the house.

Let's see what happened in this situation, following the outline in Step 1 of Chapter 3.

What did the parent actually observe?	Heard Sonja yell, saw Kael leave room unhappy.
What did the parent assume?	Sonja was behaving in her usual bossy way that always drove children away.
How did the parent feel?	Frustrated, angry, sorry for Kael.
How did the parent immediately react?	Interfered, blamed Sonja, told her what to do.
How did the child respond?	Cried, blamed mother, reacted aggressively.

In this scenario, Sonja's mother reacted on impulse to interfere in a relationship in which she was not even involved. She assumed that she knew what happened and why. She took the problem over and gave them the answer as many parents do. What was the result? The situation that involved Sonja and Kael ended as an issue between Sonja and her mother. Kael disappeared.

Mother's intervention did not help her own relationship with her daughter, nor was it helpful in developing the relationship between Sonja and her friend. Problems between them are even more likely to occur, especially when they are playing in Sonja's house, since Sonja is learning that fighting and arguing with her friends is an easy way to draw in her mother's attention. Mother's takeover is indeed a hazard in the relationship between Sonja and Kael, and also Sonja and her mother.

This point is most relevant when the children involved are brothers and sisters. Fighting between siblings is a sure bet for hooking in parents, especially if there are differences in age, sex or personality of the children that parents feel are relevant. When parents take on the role of referee, they often do not have all the facts, and judge the situation on the basis of assumptions about their children and who is likely to be to blame. They then tell their children what to do about the hassles. By taking over their children's problems with each other, parents are taking over their relationships. It is no wonder that many children don't have good relationships with their siblings when they only relate to them via their parent's interventions. Because they are not encouraged, or in some cases, allowed to work out their own problems and establish the ground rules of their relationships with their brothers and sisters, they also have difficulty doing so with children outside of the family.

Guiding children with STOP THINK DO

STOP THINK DO provides caring parents who want to help their children with an alternative to taking over their children's problems and relationships with their brothers or sisters or friends. When parents help their children to use STOP THINK DO to solve problems with peers or siblings, they are guides in the process. They are not directly involved in the hassle and they do not take over the problem or its solution. They can express their concerns during the process, but final decisions are up to those involved. Their role is to navigate, not to take over the wheel or determine the destination.

Consider this alternative approach by Sonja's mother: When she heard Sonja yelling and saw Kael upset, she STOPPED herself from reacting impulsively and from being emotionally hooked in to a situation that did not involve her. Since she cares about her daughter, she THINKS that she would like to DO something to help Sonja cope better with peer conflicts like the current one with Kael. She acts as a facilitator, a helpful third person to guide Sonja and her friend through the STOP THINK DO process to find their own answers. She and Sonja have actually made up a traffic light poster for her room to remind them of the steps to follow.

STOP

Step 1. STOP, look and listen

Mother leads Kael back into Sonja's room and suggests that they STOP, look and listen to each other to work this problem out. She may need to physically cue the children into this first step by turning their face to look and listen, putting a hand on their shoulder, calling 'STOP' or pointing to the traffic light poster. When she has their attention, she asks them one at a time to state the problem, and urges them to listen to each other.

Mother asks:

> *'What is the problem?'*

Sonja responds:

> *'I'm sick of playing this game. I want Kael to come outside with me.'*

Kael responds:

> *'I like this game and Sonja messed it up.'*

Mother clarifies:

> *'It seems that Kael wants to play the game and Sonja wants him to play outside with her.'*

Step 2. Express feelings honestly

Mother asks both children:

'How do you feel about this problem?'

She encourages them to express their honest feelings about the problem and/or she puts the feelings they are showing into words for them:

'Sonja, you feel very angry because Kael wants to do something else.'
'Kael is obviously feeling upset about it.'

Another way of helping children to become more aware of other people's feelings is to ask them to put themselves in the other person's shoes and see how they would feel then:

'Sonja, how would you feel if you were Kael and someone messed up the game you were enjoying?'
'Kael, how would you feel if someone came to play with you and then wanted to do their own thing?'

Again, help the children put their feelings into words.

THINK

Step 3. THINK of solutions

Mother suggests that they now use their good brains and think up as many answers as they can to solve this problem. Mother asks both children:

'What could you do to solve the problem?'

If they are reluctant to give ideas, mother suggests solutions, as possibilities. All suggestions are accepted without criticism or judgement and at least two ideas should be discussed before the children make a choice. After each solution is offered, mother says:

'Yes, that's one idea, what else could you do?'

Ideas offered by Sonja, Kael and mother may include:

> *'Kael could go home and play with his own games.'*
> *'Sonja could hide the game.'*
> *'We could make a deal: Sonja plays the game with me and then I'll play outside for a while.'*
> *'I'll tell my dad that you aren't playing fair. My dad's a policeman!'*
> *'We could forget the game and watch television.'*

At this point, we will detour from the main road to give you information that may be helpful when teaching your children how to brainstorm options and consequences at Steps 3 and 4. Generally, the solutions offered by children fall into the following categories:

    a. compromise, bargain, share;
    b. forget it, walk away, do something else;
    c. whinge to an adult;
    d. cry, sulk;
    e. physical force – hit, grab, kick;
    f. verbal force – yell, abuse, blame

When STOP THINK DO is taught to children in clinics or schools, these categories are given names a and b responses are called *Cool* (use a thumbs-up hand signal)

c and d are called *Weak* (use a thumbs-down hand signal)

e and f responses are called *Aggro* (use a clenched fist signal)

Cool, Weak and Aggro are shorthand terms to describe the various types of strategies for solving social problems: they help children identify strategies quickly. Parents may also find them useful to use at home. While you are not trying to tell your children what to THINK or DO as you guide them through the problem-solving process, you will naturally steer children towards Cool strategies (like sharing, ignoring, doing something else, compromising), since they generally have the best consequences. Aggro options usually get Aggro reactions from the other child and Weak ones usually annoy or stir up the other child. Cool strategies, on the other hand, are usually received positively by the other child and are more likely to be acceptable to both. Once children are accustomed to the STOP THINK DO process, you may shortcut Steps 3 and 4 by cueing children to find Cool ways to resolve issues, giving them the thumbs-up hand signal as a reminder. Now, let's return to the main road ...

Step 4. THINK about consequences

After each possible solution is offered (or alternatively, after a list of suggestions has been made), mother asks the children to think about the likely consequences of each solution:

'What might happen if you tried that suggestion?'

and how each child would feel if that consequence happened:

'How will you feel if that happens?'

She adds her ideas if the children are reluctant or unable to explore consequences fully. Consequences discussed may include:

Sonja:	*'If Kael goes home, I won't have anyone to play with.'*
Mother:	*'I see you feel unhappy about that.'*
	'How would you feel, Kael?'
Kael:	*'If you hide your game, I won't let you play with mine when you come to my place.'*
Mother:	*'How would you feel about that, Sonja?'*
Kael:	*'If we watch TV now, we will be in time for cartoons.'*
Mother:	*'You both seem pleased with that idea.'*

DO

Step 5. Choose a solution

Mother asks each child to choose the solution they think will have the best consequences:
'What do you think is the best solution?'

Sonja: *'I think we should see the cartoons.'*

Kael: *'Okay, but I really want to finish the game as well.*

If they don't agree on any one solution, mother suggests a compromise or encourages the children to agree on one:

'What solution do you agree to try?'

Sonja: *'Why don't we take the game into the TV room and play it during the commercials?'*

Kael: *'Okay, let's go!'*

It is important for mother to remember her role in this exercise. She is not responsible for the choice of solutions, nor the consequences that follow. Even if she feels that the solution chosen by the children will not work or is not the best one in her opinion, if they agree that they are happy to try it, she should encourage them. It is their problem and their relationship, and they will learn for next time.

Step 6. Act!

Mother optimistically urges the children to put their plan into action:

'Sounds like a good idea. Try it!'

With younger or unconfident children, mother breaks the chosen option into steps, guiding the children through each step or modelling actions for them. If the problem is solved, mother praises the children's efforts with words like 'Good thinking, children'. If hassles recur, she urges them to go back to STOP and THINK again of what they could DO to solve this problem. She reminds them that there are millions of answers if they keep using their brains to think. Alternatively, after Kael has left, mother may follow up with Sonja alone:

> *'Did you work out that problem with Kael today?'*

If she did, mother praises her efforts. If the problem was not resolved:

> *'What else could you have done?'*

Mother encourages further brainstorming of ideas that could be tried.

Guiding older children and adolescents

The approach outlined may be somewhat intrusive for older children and particularly adolescents, who often react unfavourably to direct involvement from parents while their friends are present. It may be preferable to approach the child/adolescent alone *after* a conflict with a friend or sibling has been observed, and take a less directive approach as follows:

STOP

Step 1. Clarify the problem you saw or heard

> *'I noticed you had a problem with Chris earlier today.'*

Step 2. Reflect the feelings

> *'You seemed really annoyed. Chris was not very happy either.'*

Child may or may not discuss the problem or their feelings. But the door is open. Lead into THINK.

THINK

Step 3. THINK of solutions

> *'Did you work it out?'*
> If not, *'Have you thought about what you could do?'*

This could be a good opportunity to discuss the child's goals, what they want to happen. These are likely to be revealed in the sorts of solutions they offer. Children can become aware of how their goals actually lead to conflicts with others like Chris who may have quite different attitudes and goals. As discussed earlier in this book, self-awareness is the beginning of self-control.

Step 4. THINK about consequences

If the child offers some suggestions, ask:

> *'What might happen if you tried that?'*
> *'How would you feel about that?'*

DO

Step 5. Choose a solution

> *'What do you think is best to do?'*

Step 6. Urge child to act

>'*Why don't you try it?*
>*If it doesn't work, you can always think of something else to try*'

Below is a summary of what to *say* and *do* to guide children to solve problems with others:

STOP | Step 1: | **STOP, look and listen**
Clarify the problem for the child(ren)
Ask, '*What is the problem here?*'
Or, '*I noticed you had a problem with …*'

Step 2: | **Express feelings honestly**
Ask, '*How do you feel about* (problem)*?*'
Or, '*You feel* (state feeling) *because* (state problem)'

THINK | Step 3: | **THINK of solutions**
Ask, '*What could you try to solve this problem?*'

Step 4: | **THINK about consequences**
Ask, '*What might happen then?*'
'*How would you feel then?*'

DO | Step 5: | **Choose a solution**
Ask, '*What do you choose (agree on) to do?*'

Step 6: | **Act!**
'*Try it*'. Praise efforts.
If it doesn't work,
'*Go back to STOP and THINK about what to DO.*

With practice, the process is shortcut as children begin to think and choose quickly:

STOP	*'You feel … because …'*
THINK	*'What could you try?'*
DO	*'Try it!'*
	'If it doesn't work, try something else'.

Practice

To feel what it is like being a real learner behind the wheel, step into a child's shoes and work through a problem you are having with your brother or sister, and friend in Appendix 2.

Journey's end

The STOP THINK DO journey is over, at least from the point of view of learning to drive. You have the skills, you know the rules, you have earned your licence, all you need now is practice. The same applies to your children. This is not to say that it will be easy from now on: you have old habits and impulses to overcome, new potholes to avoid, and fluctuating support from partners and children to drain your energy. Sounds like the juggling act of Peter's mother that opened this book!

But hopefully STOP THINK DO can give you the direction you need to reach the destination you want. It should make the parenting road clearer for you: you know what to say and do to improve your management skills and your relationship with your children. You know how to teach your children what to say and do to improve their social skills and their relationships. You are insuring them against potential hazards in their journey towards adulthood, and guaranteeing them a better quality of life. Isn't this what parenting is really about?

Appendix 1

PRACTICE

Imagine this situation:

> *Father is on the telephone. His children are playing in the same room. The noise level rises and he can't hear the telephone conversation. Funny how this always happens when he is on the telephone! They seem to be trying to embarrass him. He turns around and yells at them to be quiet or else they will be sorry when he gets off the phone. They quieten down for a while, only to start up again, twice as loud.*

Analyse this problem and work out how to solve it using STOP THINK DO. Ask your children and your partner to join you.

STOP

Step 1. STOP, look and listen

What did the children actually do? ....

....

What did the father assume? ....

....

How did the father feel? ....

....

How did he impulsively react? ....

....

How did the children respond? ....

....

How would you have reacted? ....

....

Would this have worked or would the problem behaviour be
reinforced? ....

....

Now return to Chapter 3 to read about the next step before trying
the next exercise.

Step 2: Express feelings honestly

Write a 'You' message that this father probably gave to his children.

....

....

Write an Angry 'I' message which he could also have given. Start with 'I' but finish with a 'You' message of blame.

'I feel............................. because you ....

....

Write an 'I' message that this father could give to his children to express his feelings of embarrassment, frustration or annoyance more honestly. Try not to mention 'you' at all when you state the problem.

'I feel............................. because.................................

....

Recall some 'You' messages you have given your child lately.

....

....

Did any of them work to solve the problem?

....

How could you restate these as 'I' messages?

....

....

Return to Chapter 3 to learn the next step before continuing this exercise.

THINK

Step 3. THINK of solutions

If this father's 'I' message did not work and the problem was still there, what could he or his children do to solve it?

Think of several possible solutions.

1. ....

2. ....

3. ....

4. ....

5. ....

Any more suggestions? ....

Back to Chapter 3 for the next step.

Step 4. THINK about consequences

Take the solutions suggested in Step 3 and write down what might happen if they tried each one, and how this father and his children might feel then.

	Likely consequences	Likely feelings
1. a	....	....
b	....	....

2. a ....

    b ....

3. a ....

    b ....

4. a ....

    b ....

5. a ....

    b ....

Return to Chapter 3.

DO

Step 5. Choose a solution

What do you think father chose to do from the list of possible solutions in Step 3?

....

What do you think the children chose to do from the list of possibilities?

....

....

Is a compromise necessary?..

What do you think they agreed to try? ....

....

Back to Chapter 3 for the final step!

Step 6. Act!

If the problem was resolved, how could father express his appreciation in an 'I' message? ....

If the agreed solution did not work, what logical consequence could father offer his children?

You may ....

....

(agreed solution)

OR you may ....

....

(alternative solution from list of possibilities at step 4, which is a consequence of not choosing to do agreed solution).

Indeed, the person on the end of the telephone needs to be patient or have children of their own!

Appendix 2

MORE PRACTICE

Imagine a situation where the parent is not directly involved but wants to help her or his children deal effectively with a problem involving other children.

> *Mother is gardening. She hears some colourful language from behind the hedge where her children, Gail, aged 13 years and John, aged 7 years, are playing basketball with the neighbours' son, Enzo, aged 12. Their voices get louder and the abuses more harsh. This has been going on for a while. Mother wants to help her children to deal more effectively with such situations.*

Imagine that you are Gail or John. Mother approaches you. She guides you through the STOP THINK DO steps to help resolve this problem so you relate better with each other and your friend. Record your responses to her guidelines. Ask your children to share this exercise with you. They take the roles of other children in the story.

STOP

Step 1. Mother asks, *'What is the problem here!'*

Your response ....

....

Brother/Sister's response ....

....

Friend's response ....

....

Step 2. Mother asks, *'How do you feel about it?'*

Your response ....

....

Brother/Sister's response ....

....

Friend's response..

....

OR mother puts the apparent feelings of the children into words.

THINK

Step 3. Mother asks, *'What could you try to solve this problem?'*

Your ideas:

1. ....

2. ....

Brother/Sister's ideas:

3. ....

4. ....

Friend's ideas:

5. ....

6. ....

Step 4. Mother asks, *'What might happen if you tried these ideas?'*
and *'How would you feel then?'*

Ideas	Likely Consequences	Feelings
1.		
2.		
3.		
4.		
5.		
6.		

DO

Step 5. Mother asks, *'Which option do you choose?'*

Your choice..

....

Brother/Sister's choice..

....

Friend's choice ....

....

If a compromise is needed, mother says, *'What do you all agree to try?'*

Compromise choice ....

....

Step 6. Mother says, 'Try it! If it doesn't work, try something else.'

Later, Mother discusses with you how things worked out and what else you could try.

Appendix 3

FURTHER READING

Petersen, L. & Adderley, A. (2002). *STOP THINK DO Social Skills Training: Early years of schooling ages 4–8*. Australian Council for Educational Research, Camberwell, Victoria, Australia.

Petersen, L. & Adderley, A. (2002). *STOP THINK DO Social Skills Training: Primary years of schooling ages 8–12*. Australian Council for Educational Research, Camberwell, Victoria, Australia.

Petersen, L. & LeMessurier, M. (2000). *STOP and THINK Friendship video package*. Foundation Studios, Adelaide, South Australia.

Website: www.stopthinkdo.com

Above resources available from the Australian Council for Educational Research.

The Australian bestseller that explores the delights, frustrations and dilemmas facing parents of adolescents

From the serious (relationships, depression, youth suicide) to the not-so-serious (pocket money, homework, parties), author and clinical psychologist Andrew Fuller offers practical solutions to common problems drawn from parents, their children and his own experience as a family therapist.

Full of insight, humour and good advice, this revised edition includes a new chapter on the 'Click and Go' generation. *Raising Real People* is a must-have guide for all parents of teenagers.

'Fuller is no stereotypical clinical psychologist. He has an open, down-to-earth approach to his subject, talking freely and knowledgeably in a conversational manner. 9/10'

Sunday Magazine

In *Raising Real People*, Fuller draws on wisdom accumulated from workshops, research conducted across Australia, and many successful first-hand approaches by parents to present ways to promote resilience in their children and harmony in the home.'

Age

ABOUT THE AUTHOR

Andrew Fuller has spent many years working with young people and their parents. He has developed parenting workshops for schools, local communities and private practice, and is a lecturer in the doctoral program at La Trobe University. He is also the author of *From Surviving to Thriving: Promoting Mental Health in Young People* (ACER Press, 1998). Andrew is the father of two children.